*Sideswiped by Eternity*

# *Sideswiped by Eternity*

## SERMONS FROM EBENEZER BAPTIST CHURCH

Dr. Joseph L. Roberts Jr.

Westminster John Knox Press
LOUISVILLE • LONDON

*Book design by Drew Stevens*
*Cover design by designpointinc.com*
*Cover art courtesy of Dr. Joseph L. Roberts Jr. and Ebenezer Baptist Church*

*First edition*
Published by Westminster John Knox Press
Louisville, Kentucky

This book is printed on acid-free paper that meets the American National Standards Institute Z39.48 standard. ♾

PRINTED IN THE UNITED STATES OF AMERICA

06 07 08 09 10 11 12 13 14 15—10 9 8 7 6 5 4 3 2 1

Library of Congress Cataloging-in-Publication Data is on file at the Library of Congress, Washington, D.C.

ISBN-13: 978-0-664-22970-2

ISBN-10: 0-664-22970-0

To the late Mrs. Wilhemina Colston,
Professor of History at Knoxville College,
and to my beloved wife and parents
Esther Jean Roberts
and
the late Dr. and Mrs. Joseph L. Roberts Sr.

# *Contents*

# *Introduction*

## A Letter of Liberation

Martin Luther King Jr. left a timeless legacy that speaks to us now as urgently as when he articulated his words. It has been my privilege and mission as pastor of his former pulpit in Atlanta, Ebenezer Baptist Church, to continually lift up the theological and ethical principles he and Jesus Christ embodied to build peace and equality in our community and our nation.

Dr. King's tragic death in 1968 robbed us of his sharing the practical ways we can continue to overcome. Overcoming is essentially a twofold task: empowering people to recognize their spiritual gifts and providing resources to support their journey. I believe that in Jesus Christ we have already overcome. That's the hope Martin had. It's the guarantee that we can propel ourselves into the future; Jesus Christ delivered to us the liberating gospel. Martin gave us practical ways to clear some of the hurdles blocking our way to political and social freedom. In their ever-visible footprints, I present this collection of sermons and reflections to help us face a variety of contemporary, societal, and personal challenges, and in his spirit, seek some additional ways to overcome.

When I came to Ebenezer in 1975, the church needed to catch up with Dr. King. We were perhaps focused on our proud history and probably neglecting present challenges that Dr. King would have had us addressing, if he were still with us.

First, we realize it is our responsibility to stay true to Dr. King, for he first and foremost was a servant of Jesus Christ whose gospel he preached and practiced. I stretch folks by bringing into our worship hymns and theologians from other expressions of faith. I bring to the pulpit my desire to educate and liberate. I invite our congregation to take a look at issues and make informed judgments. But always in taking a position, we are bonded by peace and nonviolence to stay true to Dr. King. Martin maintained a surgical distinction that I think is critically important: he would say, "Even though I disagree with you, your personhood is sacred to me, and I have to love you."

But first we need to know and understand him.

King's teachings are prophetically pertinent almost four decades after his assassination. The tragedy of our nation today, however, is that we are still polarized into "us" and "them." But now *we* are the superpower, and *they* are the enemy (Iraq, North Korea). Even among our own countrymen, we are aggressive and out for ourselves with little regard for others. We resolve conflict through combative confrontations at a time when we need healing, reconciliation, and community.

As individuals, we isolate ourselves. We steer into our garages, zone out in front of the Internet or television, and bury ourselves in the never-ending list of to-dos. It takes great tragedy or celebration to bring us together. We have the desire to be a community, but the connectors are missing.

Church is our connector. Church is our community. But the church's role has evolved with the times. The church is now a role model for fragmented families with pieces missing as well as a surrogate family member. We are an anchor in a world searching desperately for answers. But one of the dangers of religion today is that some churches offer black-and-white answers, allowing for no ambiguity, no debate, no questioning. Concreteness, without tolerance for reflection or critique, gives a false sense of security; it is by no means a comprehensive answer and is rarely, if ever, soul food.

The struggle that religious leaders face is between our desire to satiate the appetite of our people for security and staying true to the issues of justice and peace. These latter values are not openly espoused by media, politicians, and public figures. So we have a challenge on our hands. Religion today is pushed by "need theology"—what do we want? What do I want? We look for gratification now, and we don't want it to cost too much. Our youth know the price of everything, but the value of nothing. But Jesus Christ promises us not things, but liberation. God, through Jesus, connects us back to the God in all of us. Our deliverance is that we can face our sins and still be saved.

At Ebenezer, we are gathered from disparate backgrounds, experiences, and beliefs. But we are the church of God who includes us all. Dr. King imbued us with the ideal of inclusiveness. We believe ourselves to be a church for all nations. I have endeavored to push us to be large enough to proclaim and live out this gospel, whatever situation—personal or corporate—we encounter.

Violence, of course, is never the answer. We can disagree, but nonviolence will lift us all up to a higher level of transformed living. We continue to discover ways to overcome conflicts; through love, individually and collectively, we find peace, renewal, and strength. I hope we, as a community and as a nation, will not be locked in a mold that prevents us from thinking and acting outside traditional patterns. That would be an indictment of Martin's values and a dishonor to God.

# Part 1
## *Where Are We?*

We are a nation in crisis, on international as well as local levels. On a global scale, we are fighting HIV and AIDS; we are having to stomach a government that lies to us; and we suffer from both the arrogance of power and the arrogance of ignorance. We lack sufficient knowledge of other cultures, as well as ways to interact with those different from our own, and we have an inflated superpower mentality. But how super is that power when our country is eroding economically and spiritually?

We are in a bind, and we don't know how to get out of it. How do you deal with the grief and pain of a people suffering from unwarranted deaths and unjustifiable wars? We're fighting terrorism in the name of patriotism while our parents are brutalizing their own children. It's no surprise that a depressed malaise has settled over our nation.

From the pulpit I see crises also in the pews. One of the crises we face is not knowing where we're going to hitch our wagons. We are all trying to find and hold onto a solid base for choosing our direction in life. We wonder what does God say to us that helps us determine our choices? And how do I as pastor uphold Christian standards without imposing my own biases on the congregation? I think the answer lies in revealing the riches of biblical passages, for their multifaceted and nuanced stories are uncannily contemporary.

The ancient sages still give guidance to our contemporary society, but will we take up a cross? We say, "I don't want to give up anything, but what can I acquire? God owes me." We have no thought of the cost of redemption, no thought of being a sinner, saying, "I want to forgive myself, but I don't need God to forgive me." It doesn't work that way. We do not act without consequence. We are not purposeless. We are, rather, purposeful and certain. We are made in the image of God, and there are undebatable standards we must hold on to. We are produced by God and yet we still say to him, "I don't like the way you did it." I'm worried we have lost our standards and our values.

We suffer from spiritual obesity. We get what we want whether or not it leads to a balanced diet. We are fat Americans, and our gluttony is spiritual and psychological as well as physical. We cull what we want from our spiritual feedbag, and we avoid anything that is too challenging to digest. We feel our prize ought to be at the top of the Cracker Jack box—that we shouldn't have to work for it.

Individually and communally we face challenges that are new to our generations. Many of the families in Ebenezer are single-parent families. Missing parents leave children bereft. We face challenges to the nuclear family in the future. How will it exist, and how will children have role models if their parents are missing? And what about those parents who end up alone and unhappy?

What we have to learn to do is to decide prayerfully to affirm ourselves and to love ourselves without destroying our neighbor. If we don't love ourselves, we will take any cheap offer without scrutinizing whether or not it is truly good. We don't need love from one who is unworthy, for even with that love we will still feel the pangs of loneliness. But we are comforted in the truth that being alone with God is never being lonely.

We desire security for our nation, and we seek security for ourselves and our families. While we may find temporary solace in superficial solutions, abiding healing and comfort come from foundational, bedrock sorts of truths. There is unexpected and transforming power and humanity in community. We were not designed to live fully as solo beings. Full lives are made so and enriched by compassionate and honest relationships and connections, and by living lives united in common purpose. While we redesign new traditions and new standards, our connectedness with God and with each other gives us the strength to endure tragedy and the fortitude to move mountains.

In the following sermons, we begin by reviewing some of Dr. King's theological insights regarding events that transpired during the civil rights era in the 1960s. Notice how open he was to the guidance of the spirit of God, working through others, during the time of his leadership. He listened first, meditated and reflected deeply, then suggested several roads we may travel as we journey toward justice and equality in the nation and world.

But many in our nation resisted Dr. King's teachings, because he called for behavioral changes we have only begun to practice. Our attitudes have not been altered terribly much. Though we made some strides forward in our nation, racism is still alive and well, almost forty years after Dr. King's sacrificial death.

Moving beyond Dr. King (but not beyond the implications of his teachings), we have forfeited many of the glorious values that were the foundation stones of our republic. Dr. King continually pointed out our apostasies. Forty years beyond his life, we may not be malicious people, but we are indeed a very self-centered people. In recent years, we have noticed the ground eroding under our feet. We have no consensus on moral principles. Additionally, we have trouble defining moralism, save narrowly. We were confronted by the devastation of terrorism (September 11, 2001). When we think of the terrible tragedy that destroyed so many innocent citizens of our nation, we must confess that our nation, through some of its foreign and economic policies, is partially responsible for this drastic hostility inflicted upon us.

Yet God has been amazingly merciful and tolerant toward our nation. He has shown us a more excellent way. In moments after this tragedy, we learned that living "in community" and caring for each other may deliver our nation and our world from further disaster. Perhaps we may yet discover (through tragedy) clues that may move us toward wholeness someday. We shall overcome!

# *How Shall We Overcome?*

> "These things I have spoken unto you, that in me ye might have peace. In the world ye shall have tribulation: but be of good cheer; I have overcome the world."
>
> —John 16:33 KJV

> "He that loveth father or mother more than me is not worthy of me: and he that loveth son or daughter more than me is not worthy of me. And he that taketh not his cross, and followeth after me, is not worthy of me. He that findeth his life shall lose it: and he that loseth his life for my sake shall find it."
>
> —Matthew 10:37–39 KJV

"Be of good cheer, I have overcome the world." Isn't that almost unbelievably wonderful news? He has overcome the world!

This isn't shallow optimism, for Jesus was never naïve. He knew how rough it is for us to choose rightly and then stick by our choices come hell or high water. He knew holding such resolve is always dangerous. It never will be easy to overcome the world. We shall overcome? How shall this be? we ask.

For each one of us, this question poses a test of both our moral clear-sightedness and our strength of character. How shall we overcome the world? Somehow our Lord overcame the world, but can we? Each of us in our own time is forced to struggle to answer this question. It was the momentous and tormenting query Dr. Martin Luther King Jr. faced so nobly during his short but magnificently prophetic ministry among us.

How shall we overcome someday? In this sermon I strive to give Dr. King's answer to this rock-bottom, dead-serious question of his time and ours.

In his speech titled "Love, Law, and Civil Disobedience," Dr. King provides the context for our thinking. In 1963 he was faced with students who wanted to continue the Freedom

Rides even after they had been brutally assaulted. He was reluctant to have them continue the rides. Dr. King met all night with leaders of the movement, the group finally painfully concluding that the Freedom Rides must continue in spite of the danger to young riders. He later reflected on that night of agonizing decision:

> I remember the first group got ready to leave, to take a bus for Jackson, Mississippi, we all joined hands and started singing together. "We shall overcome, we shall overcome." And something within me said, now how is it that these students can sing this, they are going down to Mississippi, they are going to face hostile and jeering mobs, and yet they could sing, "We shall overcome." They may even face physical death and yet they could sing, "We shall overcome." Most of them realized that they would be thrown into jail, and yet they could sing, "We shall overcome, we are not afraid!" Then something caused me to see at that moment the real meaning of the movement. That students had faith in the future. That the movement was based on hope. That this movement had something within it that says somehow even though the arc of the moral universe is long, it bends toward justice. And I think this should be a challenge to all others who are struggling to transform the dangling discords of our Southland into a beautiful symphony of brotherhood. There is something in this student movement which says to us, that we shall overcome. Before the victory is won, some may have to get scarred up, but we shall overcome. Before the victory of brotherhood is achieved, some will maybe face physical death, but we shall overcome. Before the victory is won, some will lose jobs, some will be called communists and reds, merely because they believe in brotherhood, some will be dismissed as dangerous rabblerousers and agitators merely because they are standing up for what is right, but we shall overcome.
>
> That is the basis of this movement. . . .[1]

Remember the words of Jesus spoken similarly two thousand years earlier: "*These things I have spoken unto you that in me ye might have peace. In the world ye shall have tribulation: but be of good cheer; I have overcome the world*" (John 16:33 KJV). The Freedom Riders' motivation might also be found in those other words of Jesus quoted earlier, for they understood them: ". . . *and he that taketh not his cross, and followeth after me, is not worthy of me*" (Matt. 10:38 KJV).

Dr. King's book *Where Do We Go from Here: Chaos or Community?* was written at a time of great stress in his life. There were voices of dissent in the civil rights movement, challenging the efficacy of nonviolence and calling for actions that would destroy the enemy rather than the falsehood the enemy espoused.

One can sense in the book the intermingling of tension and power. The movement was at the crossroads. In the words of Charles Dickens in *A Tale of Two Cities*, "These were the best of times, and these were the worst of times."

It was August 6, 1965. The Voting Rights Bill was being signed by Lyndon Baines Johnson at the White House. This bill was of great significance because after a century of denial by terror and evasion it finally put the ballot in our hands. The Voting Rights Bill emerged out of the violence of Selma, Alabama, where, as Dr. King wrote, "A stubborn sheriff handling Negroes in the southern tradition had stumbled against the future."[2]

A lot of us are like that sheriff. We are not ready for the future. In fact, we try to resist it and find that we can't, and we stumble against the future. The sheriff stumbled against the future at the Edmund Pettus Bridge, teargassing and beating marchers to the ground. The nation exploded in righteous indignation, and fifty thousand blacks and whites joined together to march fifty miles through Alabama and arrive at the state capital of Montgomery to demonstrate disenfranchisement. The inability to vote would no longer be tolerated.

President Lyndon B. Johnson, who had already helped us greatly, addressing a joint session of Congress and a television audience of millions, described the Selma march as a modern Concord, and declared that the national government must by law ensure for every Negro the full rights of citizenship. He then pledged that we shall overcome.

But how were we to overcome? Remember, these were both the best of times and the worst of times. Let me share a little of the worst.

One year later (1966) in a Chicago suburb, some of those who had been present at the Capitol Voting Rights ceremony were jeered by rock- and bottle-throwing mobs who burned automobiles. Almost one thousand jeered them, many waving Nazi flags. One year after the Voting Rights Bill of '65 was signed. How shall we overcome?

One year later, Negro leaders who were at the ceremony were denounced and some were removed from office by their own people, a sign that tactics had changed. How shall we overcome?

One year later, white backlash became an emotional electoral issue in California, Maryland, and elsewhere.

One year later, in several southern states, men long regarded as political clowns had become governors, their magic achieved with a witches' brew of bigotry, prejudice, half-truths, and whole lies, according to Dr. King.

These were the best of times, and certainly the worst of times. How were we to overcome?

During the very same year (1965) white and Negro civil rights workers were murdered in several southern communities, and the justice system responded with swift and easy acquittals for most of those responsible for these murders. King wrote, "Many of us wept at the funeral services for the dead and for democracy."[3]

Watts went up in flames. In this irrational burst of rage, people sought to say something, but the flames blackened both them and their oppressors.

Most devastating was the judgment call of *Ramparts* magazine. In 1965 after the Voting Rights Bill was passed into law and the backlash started, its writers declared, "The black American in Harlem, Haynesville, Baltimore, and Bogalousa is worse off now than ten years ago. The Movement is in despair because it has been forced to recognize that the Negro revolution is a myth."[4] The Negro revolution is a myth. We shall overcome. But how, how shall we overcome?

Well, Jesus had said, "In this world ye shall have tribulation," and we certainly did.

Dr. King did not accept the pessimist's verdict that the Negro revolution was a myth. Instead, he used the accusation as an occasion to analyze our progress step by step to see where we were and how we got to wherever that was.

The president had specifically said, "We shall overcome." How had this opportunity been fumbled by the nation, if it had indeed?

Was the civil rights movement in despair? After Selma and the Voting Rights Act of 1965, why was widespread sympathy with the Negro revolution abruptly submerged in indifference in some quarters or banished by outright hostility in others? Why were the leaders of the movement in sharp disagreement, fighting each other more often than staying in focus together, moving toward a common goal?

The oversimplified answer is: Negroes rioted in Watts, the voice of Black Power was heard throughout the land, and the white backlash was therefore born. The white public had become infuriated, and sympathy for black causes evaporated.

But Dr. King saw more than this. This nation he realized could not overcome because it was unwilling to move from decency to equality. The watershed event was Selma, Alabama. With Selma and the Voting Rights Act of 1965, one very important phase in the civil rights revolution came to an end. A new phase opened, but few observers realized it or were prepared for its implications.

For the vast majority of the U.S. citizens, the previous decade, which King called the first phase of the movement, had been a struggle to treat the Negro with a degree of decency, not equality. Decency, not equality. Whites and blacks saw this differently.

White America was ready to demand that the Negro be spared the lash of brutality and coarse degradation, but it had never been truly committed to helping him out of poverty, exploitation, and all other forms of discrimination. This is the reason Dr. King took on economic issues, and by so doing, legitimated our involvement in this dialogue.

We wanted to move beyond decency. We looked for the second phase, the realization of equality, but we found that many of our white allies had quietly disappeared.

King wrote: "We had taken the president, the press, and the pulpit at their word when they spoke in brave terms of freedom and justice."[5] But that is the point. That is the reason we didn't make it from step one to step two, and we are still struggling with this. King wrote: "But the absence of brutality and unregenerate evil is not the presence of justice. To stay murder does not mean that we ordain brotherhood."[6]

After Selma and the high expectations of the Voting Rights Act, the word had been broken. The free-running expectations of the Negro crashed into the stone walls of white resistance. The result was havoc.

Blacks felt cheated, especially in the North, while many whites felt blacks had gained so much that it was impudent and greedy for them to ask for more so soon. It was precisely at Selma in 1965 that King saw the paths of black-white unity had to be based on the fulfillment of equality. And in the absence of agreement, the paths began inexorably to move apart.

Laws were passed in the crisis mentality after Birmingham and Selma, but no substantial fervor survived the formal signing of legislation. The recording of the law in itself was treated as the reality of the reform. King wrote: "White America, in the time of change, deals with an inner conflict as the nation passes from opposing extremist behavior to the deeper and more pervasive elements of equality. White Americans reaffirm their bonds to the status quo. White Americans had contemplated comfortably hugging the shoreline but now fear that the winds of change are blowing it out to sea."[7]

As Dr. King said, the cost of change had been cheap up until Selma. It cost no new taxes for Negroes to share lunch counters, libraries, parks, hotels, or other facilities with whites. Voter registration required neither financial nor psychological sacrifice.

The real costs lie ahead, Dr. King taught. The discount education long given blacks will, he warned, in the future have to be purchased at full price if quality education is to be realized. And the violence in our schools will have to cease. He would see this violence as a spiritual problem in our schools today.

Jobs are harder and costlier to create than voting rolls. The real costs lie ahead. The eradication of slums and housing missions is complex, far beyond integrating buses and lunch counters. In 1966, assistant director of the Office of Economic Opportunity Hyman Bookbinder said it would take one trillion dollars to fix the problem. He was not overawed by this figure. What was the solution, according to Bookbinder? "The poor can stop being poor if the rich are willing to become even richer at a slower rate."

Bookbinder went on to declare: "Unless a substantial sacrifice is made by the American people, the nation can expect further deterioration of the cities, increased antagonism between races and disorders in the streets."[8]

What was the basic difference in understanding?

"Negroes," writes King, "have proceeded from a premise that equality means what it says and they have taken white Americans at their word when they talked of it as an objective. But most whites in America in 1967, including many persons of good will, proceeded from a premise that equality is a loose expression for improvement. White America is not even psychologically organized to close the gap. Essentially, it seeks only to make it less painful and less obvious, but in more respects to retain it."[9]

Dr. King admitted that this characterization is necessarily general and that there were whites who genuinely wanted authentic equality. Their commitment was real, sincere, and expressed in a thousand deeds.

But they were balanced at the other end of the pole by the unregenerate segregationists who declared that democracy is not worth having if it involved equality. As King wrote, "Frustration and loss of confidence resulted." How shall we overcome? He gives us some clues—some truths to help us find a way out.

First, remember that the line of progress is never straight. For a period, a movement may follow a straight line, and then it encounters obstacles and the path bends. So Dr. King could understand that after Selma, there was the inevitable counter-revolution that succeeds every period of progress. Failing to understand this as a normal process of development will cause unjustified pessimism and despair. As you focus on the ultimate goal and discover it is still distant, you think no progress at all has been made.

King's second truth: A final victory is an accumulation of many short-term encounters. To lightly dismiss a cause because it does not usher in a complete order of justice is to fail to comprehend the process needed to achieve full victory, to underestimate the value of confrontation, and to dissolve the confidence born of a partial victory by which new efforts are powered.

Northern victories were not there. The aim of Dr. King was to hit racism at its heart. And the movement in the South had profoundly shaken the entire edifice of segregation.

How have we overcome?

For hundreds of years, blacks had striven to stay alive by developing an endurance to hardship and heartbreak. But in the civil rights movement, he no longer would endure; he would resist and win. Dr. King wrote: "He still had the age-old capacity to live in hunger and want, but now he banished these as his lifelong companions. He could tolerate humiliation and scorn, but now he armed himself with dignity and resistance and his adversary tasted the gall of defeat."[10]

For the first time in our history we did not have to use subterfuge as a defense or solicit pity. Our endurance was employed not as a compromise with evil, but in order to supply the strength to crush it.

The black person comes out of the civil rights struggle integrated only slightly in the external society but powerfully integrated within. This victory always has to precede all others. Black people did overcome, forcing government to write new laws to alter some of the cruelest injustices that affected us. We made an indifferent and unconcerned nation rise from the lethargy, recognize our oppression, and struggle with a newly aroused conscience. We gained manhood in a nation that had always called us "boy."

These were the values the students wanted to achieve in the Freedom Rides, that enlivened hope, even in the face of sluggish progress. Black people were no longer the *subject* of change. They were the active *organs* of change. We powered the drive and set the pace. But great victories are not won in a war for the transformation of a whole people without total participation. Dr. King gave us the prescription. He advocated that we maintain unwavering determination, dignity, and discipline.

*Preached January 16, 1994*

# *Hearing and Understanding Dr. King*

"Why do you not understand what I say? It is because you cannot accept my word."

—John 8:43

Once again we are afforded an opportunity during the celebration of Dr. King's birth to take a careful and penetrating gaze at the richness of his mind and spirit, which still lavish great blessings on us. And once again, I would commend his own books to you rather than the commentary of others. To strive to understand Dr. King without reading his own words is like trying to understand Scripture without reading the Bible.

We all must do some diligent homework to understand Dr. King, but rest assured, my sisters and brothers, the reward to us more than justifies the time we spend revisiting Dr. King's keen analysis, deep thoughts, and sensitive spirit.

And it is especially incumbent upon those who sat under his influence three decades ago, or who sit in this particular church now, to have much more than a casual acquaintance with Dr. King's immense world of mind and spirit. Others rightfully expect more knowledge of Dr. King from the members and pastor of Ebenezer. This shall forever be true, and I welcome the challenge.

We read, hear about, and strive to understand the divine forces that fueled the fires of his devotion to God, and his passion that God's righteousness be exhibited throughout the whole inhabited world and among all the people, great and small, rich and poor, of all colors and cultures, class distinctions and categories. For there is no other way to be worthy of his great legacy. If we do not diligently and constantly pursue knowledge about Dr. King through reading his books, others will take the privilege from us, as they should. He is too rich to be ignored, especially by those to whom many of his messages were addressed.

But his message has broader implications, and I submit that Dr. King does not belong to Ebenezer, or to any institution exclusively. Quite the contrary. As Edwin Stanton said of Abraham Lincoln, so we can say of Martin King, "Now he belongs to the ages."

Each year I try to reread one of his books and let his truths seep into my mind and spirit. This year is no exception. Therefore we will use as inspiration for this message his book written in 1963 titled *Why We Can't Wait!* Read it or one of his books this week, and you shall discover, as I did, that though the book was written almost thirty years ago, its message needs to be lifted up again, so the relevance of his words for our present struggles may become self-evident.

My thesis simply is this: Nations have always had a difficult time hearing and understanding prophets sent to them. But even more devastating, nations have a difficult time hearing and understanding God when he speaks to us in the person of Jesus Christ. It was from Jesus that Dr. Martin King received both the spark that ignited his torch and divine fuel for the maintenance of the eternal flame of his life. And so he continues to live among us today.

There are similarities between Jesus Christ and Martin King. Jesus started a revolution two thousand years ago, and Martin King started a national revolution forty-two years ago. We shall explore a few similarities and differences between these two revolutions. I will begin with Dr. King and work back to his inspiration and source of strength, always principally and primarily Jesus Christ.

Notice initially that both Martin King and Jesus Christ were sent into a violent world, and they both revolted against the violence they saw, in which each was forcibly enmeshed. They were both rejected by their peers. Both died, but Jesus arose to be available to save Martin King and us, and to give us eternal life. In this Jesus proves his superiority to all prophets who ever lived before or after him. Jesus is unique and singular. *There is none other name under heaven given among men, whereby we must be saved* (Acts 4:12 KJV).

Throughout this message I am going to quote the words of Jesus found in John 8:43, for they are the thread that binds the beads of this message together: "*Why do you not understand what I say?*" And Jesus answers his own question, "*It is because you cannot accept my word.*"

The year is 1963. The book is titled *Why We Can't Wait!* Dr. King's major thesis was a defense of the potency of nonviolent direct action, illustrating how it had succeeded in Birmingham and other southern cities.

Dr. James Washington of Union Theological Seminary has written regarding *Why We Can't Wait!* that Dr. King's message of nonviolence sounded like "the voice of a lonely prophet crying in a wilderness of hate and violence during the closing days of 1963."[11] Consider what had so recently transpired: On November 22, 1963, the president of the United States, John Fitzgerald Kennedy, had been cut down by an assassin's bullets. And what was Dr. King's reaction to President Kennedy's assassination? Listen to him as he speaks to us from this work:

> We were all involved in the death of John Kennedy. We tolerated hate; we tolerated the sick simulation of violence in all walks of life; and we tolerated the differential application of the law, which said that a person's life was saved only if we agreed with that person's views. . . .
>
> This may explain the cascading grief that flooded the country in late November. We mourned a man who had become the pride of the nation, but we grieved as well for ourselves because we knew we were sick.[12]

A strong indictment. I don't know whether America could take it forty-two years ago, or can even take it today.

But there was also another cause for grief during the fall of 1963. Four little innocent black girls were murdered as they attended Sunday school at the Sixteenth Street Baptist Church, when the church was bombed in September 1963.

This seemed like the end, and Dr. King was there. He eulogized the girls, weeping with those who wept, and mourning with those who mourned, and there were many.

These little girls were not controversial. They had led no marches, made no speeches, participated in no demonstrations. They were doing what anybody should be able to do in America. They were going to church on Sunday morning.

But even the sanctuary was not a safe haven thirty years ago, as we ourselves discovered on that dark June Sunday in 1974 at Ebenezer Church when the wife of Dr. King Sr. and the mother of Dr. King Jr. was assassinated in this sanctuary during morning worship. Why was the church bombed in Birmingham? Because some adults did not want to understand what Dr. King was saying?

No, more truthfully, they understood; they just did not agree with Dr. King's creed of nonviolent resistance. Can we hear his words in 1993? Violence is still around us. Everywhere. There were more black boys and men ages fifteen to twenty-five killed in one hundred hours in this nation in 1992 than were killed in one hundred days of our Persian Gulf War.

But let's not get ahead of the story.

Forty-two years ago, Dr. King wrote about the Negro revolution in 1963:

> For the first time in the long and turbulent history of the nation, almost 1,000 cities were engulfed in civil turmoil, with violence trembling just below the surface. . . . A submerged social group, propelled by a burning need for justice, lifting itself with sudden swiftness, moving with determination and a majestic scorn for risk and danger, created an uprising so powerful that it shook a huge society from its comfortable base.[13]

And the Negro revolution caught the nation off guard. Dr. King put it this way: "If room-size machines turned human, burst from the plants that housed them and stalked the land in revolt, this nation could not have been more amazed."[14]

Black people had been an object of sympathy on the part of well-meaning white people, but the nation counted on us to quietly endure, silently suffer, and patiently wait, Dr. King observed.

America was shocked and surprised by our revolution. "Just as lightning makes no sound until it strikes, the Negro revolution generated quietly . . . but when it struck, the revealing flash of its power and the impact of its sincerity and fervor displayed a force of frightening intensity."[15]

As Dr. King pointed out, however, three hundred years of humiliation and abuse could not be expected to find voice in a whisper. The storm clouds did not release a "gentle rain from heaven" but a whirlwind that has not yet spent its force or attained its full momentum. Listen to him and understand what is going on even now in our nation. Dr. King gave us glimpses of things he would not live to see but about which he could accurately prophesy.

Why did the Negro revolution happen in 1963? Why did we, so long ignored, so long written out of the pages of history books, tramp a declaration of freedom with our marching feet across the pages of newspapers, magazines, and on television screens?

What happened? Dr. King tells us: "Sarah Turner closed the kitchen cupboard and went into the streets. . . . John Wilkins shut down the elevator and enlisted in the nonviolent army. . . . Bill Griggs slammed the brakes of his truck and slid to the sidewalk. . . . The Reverend Arthur Jones led his flock in to the streets and held church in jail."

Yes, the words of parliaments, statespersons, and kings and queens did have to make room for the history-making deeds of servants, drivers, elevator operators, and ministers. "Why do you not understand what I say?" said Jesus. "It is because you cannot bear to hear my words."

Hear and understand the national revolution that began in 1963. What caused it?

First, it was precipitated by the slow pace of school desegregation. It had been nine years since the Supreme Court decision of 1954 that abolished legal segregation in education, but only 9 percent of southern blacks were attending integrated schools. At this pace, it would be 2054 before integration in southern schools would be completed.

Adding insult to injury were the Pupil Placement Laws that states were allowed to enact. If a state passed such a law, children could be placed by virtue of family background, special ability, and other subjective criteria in certain public schools. The Supreme Court, by allowing Pupil Placement Laws, made token integration acceptable, even though school segregation had been ruled illegal.

Black people felt the frustration and inequality of public education as the pendulum swung between elation when the 1954 edict was handed down and the despair that followed the failure to bring it to life.

The second reason for the outburst in 1963 was the general disappointment of black people with both national political parties. The Democratic Party had a great civil rights bill and President Kennedy espoused it. The Republicans likewise had civil rights legislation, but their candidate made no convincing argument that he would keep his party's promises.

The trouble lay here. There was a marking of time in fulfilling civil rights between 1961 and 1962. As Dr. King wrote, while some Negroes were appointed to significant jobs, and hospitality was extended to us at the White House, the dreams of the masses remained in tatters. Now, the Negro recognized the same old bone being tossed to him, but this time it was done with courtesy and it came on a silver platter. But it was the same old bone.

The third reason for the Negro revolution of 1963 was housing discrimination. It was to be wiped out "with the stroke of a pen" as soon as President Kennedy took office, but it was not. In fact, it took two years for the Kennedy administration to write an executive order on the subject, and then the problem of discrimination against people of color by lending institutions was never addressed. This problem is still alive today. It's still hard to borrow mortgage money.

The fourth reason for the Negro revolution of 1963 was the Cuban Missile Crisis of 1962. America demonstrated that it would go to any lengths to preserve freedom abroad, but was extremely weak in its concrete commitment to its own citizens of color within the boundaries of this nation.

The fifth reason was the issue of the decolonization and liberation of nations in Asia and Africa. By 1963 more than thirty-four African nations had thrown off the yoke of the colonizer for freedom. Dr. King relates this story: A group was reciting grievances to a visiting African statesperson, but finally the African leader waved a weary hand and said, "I am aware of current events. I know everything you are telling me about what the white man is doing to the Negro. Now tell me: what is the Negro doing for himself?"[16]

Finally, 1963 was the one hundredth anniversary of the Emancipation Proclamation. And there were big celebrations, thick cuts of roast beef, and legions would listen as luminous phrases were spoken to salute the great democratic landmark that 1963 represented. But President Lyndon B. Johnson said it best: emancipation was a proclamation, but not a fact. At best, emancipation was a brave start, but urgent business was still at hand. Now some of the goals of this Negro revolution were rejected and still have not been realized, but we fight on.

Dr. King relates the story of a near-death experience. He was in Harlem autographing his first book, *Stride toward Freedom*, when a woman, obviously deranged, stabbed him in the chest with a letter opener. He lay in bed at Harlem Hospital for hours while preparations were made to remove the blade from his chest. One of the chief surgeons told him afterwards the reason for their caution and long delay. The razor tip of the letter opener was so close to his aorta that if he had merely sneezed it would have punctured this main artery and Dr. King would have drowned in his own blood. They had to open his whole chest to remove the letter opener. Dr. King knew rejection, but he didn't abandon nonviolent resistance. He was a lonely prophet in a strange, cold, and violent world.

In 1963 the knife of violence was just that close to the nation's aorta. Hundreds of cities could have had thousands of deaths but for the operation of certain forces that gave political surgeons an opportunity to cut boldly and safely to remove the deadly peril.

Jesus knew rejection of a more devastating type. But he, too, never quit on us. Now, should we quit on each other? In this, Martin King and Jesus Christ were together.

Come with me now to our biblical text, the culmination of a sad set of episodes in the Gospel of John. Jesus has been rejected in both Galilee and Jerusalem. He had announced a revolution in the synagogue at Nazareth in Galilee, and he was rejected there that very day, stabbed in the back by his own people. Why did they not understand what Jesus said? Because they could not bear to hear his words.

We must endeavor to hear and understand Jesus if we are ever to hear and understand any of his prophets, priests, and apostles in our day. Why wasn't Jesus understood? The blessings Jesus bestowed were spiritual, while the blessings people craved were physical. So long as he was feeding five thousand every day they were satisfied. But when he called them to look beyond the physical bread and realize these miracles were signs of higher, spiritual gifts that could be theirs for the asking, they left him in large numbers.

In the eighth chapter of John we can trace the course of popular opinion about Jesus, which ran from a somewhat hopeful perplexity to a furious hostility that, for the first time, broke out in actual violence. It all started so simply. Jesus got into trouble for healing a man on the Sabbath day. He had to hide to escape their violence, but he didn't quit. He kept preaching in public.

Why did this happen? There were many Jews loyal to the law and proud of their Abrahamic descent who would have enjoyed an affiliation with Jesus. But they knew that if they were to become disciples they would have to alter their outlook on many matters. It was so much easier to quibble, question, and debate, which is the reason they argued with Jesus so much. "Why do you not understand what I say? It is because you cannot hear my word."

A friend supposedly remarked to Mark Twain that there was so much in the Bible that he could not understand that it really worried him. The famous humorist is alleged to have answered, "It is not what I do not understand that worries me, but what I do understand, for it seems too very difficult to fulfill."

A university senior put it this way, "I would like to be religious, but there is so much about Jesus that I cannot believe."

The preacher answered, "Suppose I could prove to you that Jesus was truly the son of God, that I could make it so plain that you couldn't possibly doubt it. Would you then be willing to make him the master of your life?"

"I guess that's my problem," the youth replied. "I know I would have to clean up a lot of things, and I am not ready to do that."

Is America ready to do that? We have a lot of things to clean up. But Martin, Jesus, and the Father are one. They march together. Don't fight the Lord.

*Preached January 17, 1993*

# *Tempted Down from Great Living*

## NAACP Emancipation Day Address for Atlanta, January 1, 2000

> All the people said to Samuel, "Pray to the LORD your God for your servants, so that we may not die; for we have added to all our sins the evil of demanding a king for ourselves." And Samuel said to the people, "Do not be afraid; you have done all this evil, yet do not turn aside from following the LORD, but serve the LORD with all your heart; and do not turn aside after useless things that cannot profit or save, for they are useless. For the LORD will not cast away his people, for his great name's sake, because it has pleased the LORD to make you a people for himself."
>
> 1 Samuel 12:19–22

Many nations start from good beginnings. They emerge from the womb of noble aspirations. Visions and dreams initially fill the minds and hearts of a nation's citizens and leaders. Aspirations reach to lofty summits, recorded in its founding documents, its constitution, and its bill of rights. But a nation can soon be entrapped by compromise and political expediency. Hopes for great living are suddenly downsized, and dreams and visions of good and righteousness are soon tempered and greatly diminished. Nations are like individuals. Usually we start perfect at birth but then it's a downhill roller-coaster ride throughout the rest of our lives.

A few American statespersons have understood this tendency of human beings and their institutions. They have understood that all nations are tempted down from great living at one time or another. Thomas Paine, the great American patriot, understood this. Listen to this warning he delivered in a Fourth of July address during the infancy of this nation:

> Let Americans celebrate their freedoms and remember that they must be ever vigilant that those precious freedoms not

> erode through neglect or misunderstanding. . . . It is far too easy to lose them. And in this celebration, let Americans reflect on these powerful words and understand: Those who expect to reap the blessings of freedom must undergo the fatigue of supporting it.

Even more significant for African Americans are the words of our "founding father," the abolitionist and great journalist Frederick Douglass, who wrote this simple sentence: "I know of no rights of race superior to the rights of humanity."

Now, couple Frederick Douglass's words with those of Thomas Paine, and see what emerges. "Those who expect to reap the blessings of freedom must undergo the fatigue of supporting it" (Paine). "I know of no rights of race superior to the rights of humanity" (Douglass).

Allow me to bring a third witness to the stand as I argue that America has allowed itself to be tempted down from great living. Booker T. Washington, another great black American, made a critically vital contribution to humanity and the education of our people. He has at times been accused (perhaps justifiably so) of being too accommodating to the inequities his people faced. But you cannot visit the great Tuskegee University today without praising this educator and statesman for his farsighted, factually correct analysis of our need as a people, to ready ourselves to compete with anybody through the preparation of the body, mind, and spirit by bringing heart and hand together. For it was better than one hundred years ago that Booker T. Washington made this bold and prophetic statement to an all-white audience from whom he hoped to garner financial support for Tuskegee:

> No member of your race in any part of the country can harm the meanest member of mine without the proudest and bluest blood in Massachusetts being degraded. . . . When Mississippi commits crime, New England commits crime, and by so much, lowers the standard of your civilization.[17]

In other words, you cannot hold me back without holding yourselves back. You cannot hold me down without holding yourselves down. You cannot slow me down without slowing yourselves down. You cannot stop me without stopping yourselves.

Yes, many nations start from good beginnings. Visions and dreams initially fill the minds and hearts of its citizens and leaders. But it seems almost inevitable that somewhere down the line innocence flees, and nations, like individuals, are tempted down from great living.

Let us visit a reality that cannot be denied. When we think of this nation with all of the glorious memories of the past, its technological prowess in the present, and its lavish celebration of the future, we must be careful not to be caught up in a subtle snare. And what is it? Simply this: It is so easy when our economy is doing well for the American people and our leaders to believe that national greatness really consists in trade balances, productive capacity, technological improvements, and fortunate political alliances.

It is too easy to believe we are living great lives in the United States because our Gross Domestic Product growth reached 5.4 percent in 1998, well above the Federal Reserve Bank's 2.5 percent target for nondomestic output.

It is so easy to believe we are living in great times as a nation because we have the lowest interest rates in twenty-five years, combined with low inflation, relatively strong consumer demand, and a reasonable level of corporate capital investment for productivity enhancement, which suggests continued domestic economic growth in the near future.

Good news, we say. Of course it is good news. For all these factors do make a contribution to the lives of citizens. We dare not deny this, but we need to remember that all the economic good news we have cannot save life from fear, tension, futility, frustration, secularism, or disregard for the divine in our lives.

The pages of history are littered with the record of nations that have been seduced downward, that have been tempted downward from great good and godly living in prosperous times, when things seemed to be going well.

Come with me to the biblical example this morning, nestled in the twelfth chapter of the prophetic writing of Samuel.

The infant nation of Israel was just getting started on its long journey toward national prominence. But Samuel, the first prophet, was gravely concerned lest the life of this infant nation become futile and vagabond, lest it fall from its noble beginning. So he writes, "Yet do not turn aside from following the LORD, but serve the LORD with all your heart; and do not turn aside after useless things that cannot profit or save, for they are useless" (1 Sam. 12:20–22).

In other words, the prophet Samuel implies that kings, presidents, prime ministers, trade balances, productive capacity, technological improvements, even fortunate political alliances may well be those vain things that cannot profit or save. So do not turn aside from following the Lord, but serve the Lord with all your heart.

Let's bring this passage home. As a nation, we have many political, economic, and social panaceas available in our time. We lay famous names on get-well quick schemes designed to cure the nation's ills without either effort or sacrifice on the part of citizens or Christians.

But wise people refuse to give consideration to rosy-hued schemes that promise a political or economic outcome for nothing. Still, nations, churches, and individuals can be sold gold bricks and persuaded to invest in phony stock.

Nations, as well as individuals, can be led astray by fool's gold or deceived by debts that will never have to be paid. Like with our credit cards—we spend and spend and then cringe.

But let us remember anything that relieves the individual of moral responsibility, anything that turns men and women away from great living and fascinates them with petty pleasures, anything that tries to make life out of an abundance of things, is in the end both poor politics and poor morals. The remedy for these deadly ills must be found elsewhere, in the realm of the spirit.

Now the twelfth chapter of Samuel reveals that Israel, the people of God, simply wanted an earthly king. Neighboring nations all had kings. They felt peer pressure. Why shouldn't they want a king? It seems like a rather simple, innocent request on the surface, doesn't it? But it may surprise you to discover that this innocent request was a major offense, an affront to the Almighty God who had delivered them from their enemies and supplied all their needs. The question before God was this: Was he not good enough for Israel any longer?

No, we're not saying that. We just want to be self-sufficient, with our own king and our own resources.

Self-sufficiency is as American as apple pie and motherhood, but from God's point of view it is a deep offense: "Do not turn aside after useless things that cannot profit or save, for they are useless." The prophet is pleading with Israel. Remember how you came to where you are today. Don't treat God as if he is only your 9-1-1 deity, who you ring up only in times of emergency and disaster and ignore when the threat is over. This is the reason God was disappointed with Israel and is now disappointed with us.

The United States of America has turned away from the great truths of its foundations, to vain things that cannot profit or save. So we are tempted down from great living.

What is the first thing that cannot profit or save? Using people and nations will drag America down from great and righteous living. We treat people and nations as disposable. First, let me speak of Osama bin-Laden. You will perhaps remember that this nation was terribly offended in 1998 when our American embassies in Nairobi, Kenya, and Dar es Salaam, Tanzania, were bombed. Innocent American brothers and sisters and many more African brothers and sisters were killed or seriously injured. It was a tragedy. It shouldn't have happened, nor should it go unpunished.

And our nation retaliated. The United States hit back with cruise missiles in the Sudan, the largest country in Africa, and Afghanistan. And do you know who we blamed for the bombing of our embassies? Our chief suspect was Osama bin-Laden. He is a wealthy man from Saudi Arabia who is our nation's public enemy number one. But why does he dislike us so much? Osama bin-Laden was a veteran of the war against communism for twenty years. In fact, our CIA recruited him and other young

Muslims to fight Soviet troops in Afghanistan in 1979. He was our ally, on our side for twelve years, until the Persian Gulf War in 1991.

He turned against us then because we use people and nations and then dispose of them. We fall from greatness when people and nations become disposable.

The United States sent more than five hundred thousand U.S. troops into Saudi Arabia, bin-Laden's native land. Then after the American embassy bombings we sent bombers to the Sudan, to destroy chemicals we thought were being produced there to manufacture nerve gas. But we were wrong. We destroyed the Shifa Pharmaceutical Plant in Khartoum, Sudan, which produced painkillers and malaria medicine.

Bin-Laden had sizable holdings in the pharmaceutical plant in Sudan. He escaped unharmed, but his hatred for the United States grew. Yes, we fired up his animosity toward us with our bombing of the pharmaceutical factory. But at the same time he also held a monopoly on gum arabic, Sudan's leading export and a staple of much fruit juice production in the United States of America. And we have not asked our U.S. juice companies to stop buying bin-Laden's gum arabic rather than bombing his pharmaceutical factories in the Sudan: the reason we haven't is that it will hurt American juice producers. We are falling from greatness.

We are supporting Osama bin-Laden. We are helping him buy arms by keeping quiet about using his gum arabic. And here is the hypocrisy of America: this nation uses people and then cries foul when they retaliate.

This nation, under God . . . are we under God? Are we living as one nation, under God, or are we still divided?

We have normal trade relations with China—Red China—but can a nation under God really trade with China?

House Minority Leader Richard Gephardt, a Democrat, is to be commended and respected for breaking with President Clinton on the issue of trade with China. Gephardt observed that the United States has no business playing business as usual with a Chinese tyranny that persecutes Christians, Muslims, and religious leaders from many other faiths. China precludes tens of millions from practicing their religion, sells the most lethal weapons to the most dangerous of nations, profits off slave labor, and engages in the utter evil of forced abortion.

We trade with China. Are we a nation under God? Or do we justify anything for a dollar?

And while we trade with China we ignore our brothers and sisters in the Sudan, poor black people, who need foreign aid. There are 2.6 million sisters and brothers in the Sudan facing starvation. More than 350,000 died from starvation last year. The Sudan is a vast emptiness of almost 1 million square miles, a place that is home to 28.5 million Africans. A civil war has been raging in that poor country for the past fifteen years, and God's people are starving there. But we have done little or nothing to settle that dispute. And our country, under God, does not give 25 percent or even 15 percent of our budget in foreign aid. Less than 1 percent of our budget goes to foreign aid.

The Sudanese government has tried to starve rebels into submission by cutting off food aid. Two annual harvests have failed to produce food because of a dry spell. Seven hundred thousand people have nothing to eat, save what relief workers can bring in. And the government barred all relief aid to the neediest areas during February and March 1999. We dipped into Kosovo to help a civil dispute. Why not into the Sudan to help the people? We are tempted down from great living.

In Samuel's day, people worshiped other gods of the surrounding tribes and nations. In the United States some religious leaders place regional loyalty and regional bigotry above the Almighty God and his righteous rule over the nation. In 1995, the Southern Baptist Convention apologized to African Americans for "conditioning and/or perpetuating individual and systemic racism in our lifetime" and urged its members to work for racial reconciliation.

But then the South Carolina Baptist Convention withdrew its financial support of the state's Christian Action Council because the latter was involved in efforts to encourage the removal of the Confederate flag from the state capital of South

Carolina. The Christian Action Council joined Governor David Beasley in calling for the removal of the flag from the dome of the statehouse in Columbia, South Carolina.

But a Reverend Eubanks and more than a dozen other Southern Baptist Convention clergy objected to the Council in a silent vigil and march. Eubanks et al. accused the governor of creating a division among churches by making the flag controversy a moral issue. The Reverend Mr. Eubanks and others issued a position paper titled "The Moral Defense of the Confederate Flag: A Special Message for South Carolina Christians." But wait a minute. Isn't this a bit presumptuous? Are there no black Christians in South Carolina?

This kind of talk fuels the burning of black churches. When will we bury it all and let this thing go?

Yet again, we are tempted down from great living.

As we continue, individually and as a nation, our struggle for freedom and for great living, let us be ever mindful of Thomas Paine's prophetic warning: "Those who expect to reap the blessings of freedom must undergo the fatigue of supporting it." Freedom, once attained, requires vigilance to maintain it against attack, misunderstanding, and neglect. Onward we march.

# *Our Supreme Treasure*

> "Do not be afraid, little flock, for it is your Father's good pleasure to give you the kingdom."
>
> —Luke 12:32

Allow me to introduce this message, titled "Our Supreme Treasure," by lifting up a poem written by a nineteenth-century Scottish preacher, Dr. George MacDonald. Though gifted and brilliant, MacDonald lived most of his life in poverty and obscurity. He suffered from consumption but had a bright and playful disposition throughout his eighty-one years of life. And what was his secret? According to Dr. Alvin Rogness, MacDonald rested on what he called the "holy presence." Intuitively, he could see to the heart of the matter. Look at his poem "The Waiting Father."

> I see a little child whose eager hands
> Search the thick stream that drains the crowded street
> For possible things hid in its current slow.
> Near by, behind him a great palace stands,
> Where kings might welcome nobles to their feet,
> Soft sounds, sweet scents, fair sights there only go. . . .
> There the child's father lives, but the child does not know.[18]

Are we not like this child, searching in muddy streams for hidden treasure, for hidden things of value, while our heavenly father sits in the palace just behind us, waiting to give us all that is good for us? But we do not know our father is so close to us. We have overlooked him in our search.

Many of us are like this, aren't we? We spend so much of the precious time and energy God has given to us probing around for things that we hope will give us great satisfaction in life. We search many thick streams in the crowded streets of life. And what are we searching for? It may be money. It may be prestige. It may be power. It may be taking first place in life's mad race. It could be all of these.

And why do we do this? Is it not because we have a deep suspicion that somewhere in those thick streams a supreme treasure is hidden? A treasure created for all of us. A treasure fitting our deepest longings, our fondest dreams. If we could only find it.

While we are searching for this treasure, our heavenly father watches us from his palace window and shakes his head in sorrowful regret, for he had so hoped we would turn to him and see in him the supreme treasure of life. But we turn our back on him and keep running our hands through the stream.

But you see, the supreme treasure of our lives will not be discovered in the muddy waters found in the streets of our cities. Not in money, nor in prestige, or power, nor in taking first place in life's mad race. The supreme treasure of life is found in God himself.

And what did his son tell us about this? "Do not be afraid, little flock, it is your Father's good pleasure to give you the kingdom. . . . For where your treasure is, there your heart will be also" (Luke 12:32, 34).

It is at the table of the Lord's Supper that we locate much of our supreme treasure, for this table comes from heaven, from God's palace itself. Look at the cross over the table. It is our assurance that he wants us to lay claim to him, now and forever, though we are unworthy of his sacrifice for us.

In the Lord's Supper we live with God and in God, through Jesus Christ our savior. In and through this supper we enter into his palace and sit at his table and partake, though unworthy, of heavenly food. Are you hungry for the strength to do right? "This is my body, broken for you." By means of this table, Jesus assures us that we have nothing to fear. It is our father's good pleasure to give us the kingdom, not sell us the kingdom. We can't buy it, for, you see, your deliverance, your salvation and mine was no cheap thing. We were bought with a price. Somebody died so we could live.

Now the second blessing we receive in this supreme treasure is God himself. The poet T. S. Eliot penned these words, which are so true to our lives: "Most of the trouble in this world is caused by people wanting to be important."

Isn't it a glorious relief to discover that we don't have to pretend to be something or somebody other than who we are in Jesus? We are important not because of who we think we are or what the world thinks of us, but simply because God loves us and claims us as his own. This means we no longer need to fight for a place in the sun. Isn't that a glorious relief for us? "I may not be a shining star, I may not be all that you are . . . but I thank the Lord that I'm his child."

Well, let's move on and face stark reality. Muddy waters are unavoidable on the streets of our lives. Most of us have to travel through them to receive the supreme treasure of life—if we are to reach God and his kingdom.

Historian and author C. Northcote Parkinson suggests that those with great ability don't usually emerge from happy circumstances. Our ability is enhanced by an initial measure of adversity, followed by later success.

You have to go through something testing your fortitude. You will go through a lot of muddy water on your way home to God. Walter Elliott puts it this way: "Perseverance is not a long race; it is many short races one after another." When will we finish?

You'll probably never get your pot of gold at the end of the rainbow. You're going to have some muddy waters to traverse. But as you go, enjoy the small things. The common beauties, the little day-to-day events, sunshine on the fields, birds on the bough, breakfast, dinner, supper, the daily paper on the porch, a friend passing by. So many people who go afield for enjoyment leave it behind them at home.

We come closer to the supreme treasure, who is God Almighty himself, as we learn to become servants of humanity as Jesus was a servant of all. To give, we discover, is more blessed than to receive. Keep watch over yourself and over all the flock. Help people get out of the muddy water and to the palace.

Wise people do not necessarily know more facts, but they comprehend the deeper meaning of the generally known facts. They accept life as it is and focus less on personal needs and more on helping others. People are gracefully molded and matured by pain and hardship; it seems to depend on how one handles the crises when they happen.

"Fear not little flock. It is your Father's pleasure to give you the kingdom." We have his ear at all times through prayer. He comforts us in our grief. He gives us hope when we are discouraged. In the hour of death he is at our side, ready to put us on our feet again in his everlasting kingdom. God is the supreme treasure.

*Communion Meditation, November 2, 2003*

# *Sideswiped by Eternity (Part 1)*

In this precarious venture called life, we are all sideswiped from time to time by eternity. It's true, isn't it? Just think of all those near misses, those times when we have come so close to being utterly destroyed, those times we have so narrowly escaped harm and danger.

But the gears of my soul shifted this week at our Brotherhood meeting. It was a time to share the experiences of our encounters with God, to witness to our personal revelations of his presence in our lives. And what a glorious night it turned out to be. We heard testimonies from some brothers who spoke of being sideswiped by eternity in a far more positive and ennobling sense than I originally contemplated.

For you see, these brothers did not always see being sideswiped by eternity as the intrusion of danger. For them, being sideswiped by eternity has been a means of grace and goodness, bounty and joy. Being sideswiped by eternity was God's intervention on their behalf during some of the dark and dismal hours. When God sideswiped them, he brought light and hope to their souls. When God sideswiped them, he reduced to nonexistence their unemployment anxiety. Two of them related that just when they were on the brink of losing their jobs with much-needed compensation, they prayed fervently about it and suddenly God sideswiped them, not only with other jobs but with better compensation than they had before.

But then came Tuesday morning—the colossal events of heart-rending tragedy for the whole world. We watched in horror as the World Trade Center collapsed and the Pentagon was severely damaged. *Has the world gone mad*, we wondered? What we didn't believe could happen in our nation actually did happen. Thousands of innocent lives taken in an instantaneous inferno of hatred, accompanied by a meltdown of steel and shattering concrete, burning and burying so many alive.

In so many instances, they didn't know what hit them. But if they did, and could, they called up somebody to say, "It's over, but remember I love you. . . . Take care of the kids."

We were left so helpless and desolate. We wept with those whose tears were unrelieved because lives and family ties had been permanently destroyed so viciously, savagely, and violently. Tears, pain, and anguish were everywhere, and still are as loved ones sought to know whether they should wait with any hope or give up in despair. The waiting was almost worse than not knowing anything. The fallout is still with us and will not depart from our consciousness. We stayed glued to our televisions and to the telephone.

But thank God we also prayed in churches, mosques, and synagogues. Yes, the doors of God's houses were open everywhere to everyone who wanted to talk with their God and ask for divine help for loved ones and our world in this time of dire need.

Now we must find some way to interpret these events. Mind you, my interpretation is not a political analysis, for that is beyond the competence or comprehension of this preacher. Rather, there are some religious issues that we cannot duck or evade.

What does it mean to be sideswiped by eternity or immortality? We can all admit that life sometimes seems empty and purposeless, and sometimes we feel frighteningly alone. And we sometimes are.

But have you noticed this? In these very moments, often something intrudes in the midst of the lowness. Something intrudes like the call of a bird for its mate. Something intrudes reminding us that there is another dimension to life than this seemingly endless round of going to work, cashing the paycheck and paying bills, and experiencing troubles and tribulations. Something intrudes. We are sideswiped by immortality, by the eternal God.

Paul tells us something about immortality and eternity in his letter to his friends at Philippi. He is in prison, in Rome, awaiting a court hearing before the emperor. He's been waiting two years to get before the highest tribunal in the empire. He is in Rome because he could find no justice in Palestine, where the Jewish Sanhedrin condemned him for betraying them by preaching and proclaiming that Jesus Christ was the Messiah.

They were also disturbed by Paul's persuasive powers, for he preached with a boldness and intensity that were winsome and convincing far beyond their expectation. But you see, they didn't know Paul had been sideswiped by eternity, by immortality, on the Damascus road. The Jewish leaders in Palestine wanted Paul put to death, but they did not have legal authority to carry out the sentence. And Paul knew the Jewish leaders could not execute him without the approval of Rome.

So here we see the old man with failing vision, grasping a sliver of hope. He would appeal his case to Rome for he was a free Roman citizen. But he was an agitator, the Jews said. He would probably try to undermine Rome. He would probably speak against Caesar. Paul would soon try to destroy the Pax Romana, the peace of Rome.

Ah, but this call of God, this call of immortality, strengthens us to do more than just grin and bear it. It calls us to know that we have been sideswiped by immortality. We respond to the eternal and immortal that is with us and in us at this moment.

This is the first insight about immortality: you don't have to wait until you die to know that you are eternal.

You will run into somebody this week. You will bump into them—sideswipe them, if you please—with the immortal that is in you right now. You won't have to say, "Excuse me." People are glad to be sideswiped by immortals. For when you are moved to help someone you do not even know or to pray for and reach out to someone else, you have sideswiped them with the eternity God has placed in you.

This sideswiping with immortality also helps us notice and appreciate as never before the simple things: the flowers, the birds, and the hidden beauty in our lives and in others. And it helps us reach out to help others, actively help them in their struggles even if it is only with a hug.

When we are sideswiped by eternity and immortality we are involved with issues and causes that cannot be called profitable, which do not lift the bottom line and increase returns to stockholders. When we have been sideswiped by immortality we struggle to be sure that others besides ourselves are blessed with the essentials for rich and abundant life.

I read about such devotion in the *New York Times* in an article titled "Two Normal Guys Transformed." This article reported on the exemplary conduct of two men who worked for the Mays Davis Group, a small minority-owned investment bank with offices in the World Trade Center.

Mr. DeVito and Mr. Ramos helped people down the stairs and out of the building. DeVito observed that there was no gender, no race, no religion on the staircase. It was everyone helping each other. That's what it means to be sideswiped by the eternal, by the immortal: each person helping somebody else make it to safety and security if at all possible.

Mr. Ramos died helping a stranger, staying behind with him. Mr. DeVito led the other employees out just before the second tower came down. They both knew, whether they lived or died, they were the Lord's.

What is immortality?

Immortality really is a destiny because Christ is already in us. There was no gender, no race, no religion on the staircase. It was everyone helping each other. The Christ, eternity, immortality was alive in people helping each other to escape the flames and debris:

Firefighters laboring in agony for long hours without relief, and helpers coming from other firehouses all over the nation. Policemen working nonstop to save lives and evacuate people. Civilians giving first aid until ambulances could arrive. This is what it means to be sideswiped by the eternal, by the immortal within us.

A reporter hugging a distraught woman. Blood donors flooding the American Red Cross. Restaurant owners supplying free food as long as they had it. These are who sideswipe all of us with their eternal gifts of immortality.

Who will you sideswipe with eternity tomorrow on your job, in your place of authority, wherever you happen to be? Don't wait for another disaster to sideswipe somebody with your immortality.

*Preached September 16, 2001*

# *Sideswiped by Eternity (Part 2)*

Theologian P. T. Forsythe writes, "Our immortality lies on us with that kindling weight, that weight of glory, that weight of wings."[19] But it is weight, not pressure. These wings add to our weight, yet lift us from the ground. Make your weight your wings. Ask yourself this question: Am I living as an immortal being on earth at the present time or only as one who hopes to someday become immortal in heaven?

Immortality is really a destiny pressing on us now by Christ.

Yes, writes the poet, a man's reach must exceed his grasp, or what's a heaven for?

Our foreign policy and our partisan siding in Middle East disputes; our economic boycotts of so many Middle Eastern countries—we have done some things that reflect either an indifference to or a hostility toward Muslims. The Arab world feels it is not the geopolitical player it should be. Theirs was a great civilization from the seventh century on. . . .

The Arabs or Muslims were used to resist Russians in Afghanistan and then dumped—the great American betrayal. What happened at the World Trade Center and the Pentagon is horribly sinful and wrong. Heinous and without any justification. Innocent lives caught in the crossfire of bloody ideologies of the indiscriminate . . . unwarranted death and destruction. But the actions of 9/11 are not the core teachings of Islam, any more than they are of Judaism or Christianity.

In words the prophet Muhammad quoted in one of his last public sermons, God speaks thusly to all humanity: "O people! We have formed you into nations and tribes so that you may know one another, not to conquer, convert, subjugate, revile or slaughter, but to reach out toward others with intelligence and understanding."

Let us return now to Paul.

One would assume that his final imprisonment in Rome, which lasted two years, signaled the absolute end of Paul's missionary activity. But we are in for a glorious surprise. For quite the contrary, Paul's imprisonment did not diminish, but actually increased his missionary and ministerial activities. He was even more bold in his witnessing for Christ in prison than before. What did he have to lose? In fact, as William Barclay writes, Paul's bonds, his prison chains, his fetters, actually broke down barriers blocking the spread of the gospel in Rome:

> I want you to know, beloved that what has happened to me has actually helped to spread the gospel so that it has become known throughout the whole imperial guard and to everyone else that my imprisonment is for Christ; and most of the brothers and sisters, having been made confident in the Lord by my imprisonment, dare to speak the word with greater boldness and without fear.—Philippians 1:12–14

These bonds, this imprisonment, were a great boost to the gospel.

What does Paul mean by this? His tribulation provided a great opportunity to advance the gospel of Jesus Christ? We are puzzled. How is this so, Paul?

Paul's very imprisonment cleared away obstacles that would hinder the advancement of the gospel. Far from shutting the door to his missionary endeavors, God opened the way to new spheres of wonderful work and service into which Paul would never otherwise have penetrated.

Remember, Paul made his appeal to Rome after he could find no justice in Palestine among his own people. And in due time, he was dispatched to Rome accompanied by a Roman military escort. When he arrived in Rome, he was placed in the custody of the captain of the Praetorian guards. Paul was privileged. He was allowed to live in a house by himself while awaiting his day in court, although at his own expense. And he was always under the watchful eye of Rome, for a soldier was assigned to guard him at all times. Paul was allowed to have visitors come to his house, and he invited the Jews of Rome to come and discourse with him. He was not afraid to preach the word of God. He was not ashamed to stand up for God even in the face of opposition. This is what got Paul in trouble in the first place with the Jews.

But he didn't want to miss an opportunity to sideswipe them with the eternal, with the immortal God manifested in Jesus Christ the Lord. He never stopped witnessing. Nor should we. All the Praetorian Guard soon knew that Paul was in prison for proclaiming Jesus Christ as Lord. Many of these hardened soldiers were moved toward Christ by Paul's bold testimony in the face of his enemies, in the face of Roman authority. And the very news of Paul's boldness in prison gave the sisters and brothers in Philippi fresh courage to preach the gospel and witness for Christ in spite of opposition. And because of his imprisonment, many of the Christians there seemed to have lost their fear of chains.

Lose your fear of chains. Lose your fear of getting hooked up to help somebody.

The Romans were sideswiped by Paul's eternity, his immortality.

Go back to that staircase in the World Trade Center. There was no gender, no race, no religious distinctions on that staircase. It was everyone helping each other:

> It is my eager expectation and hope that I will not be put to shame in any way, but that my speaking with all my boldness, will be exalted now as always in my body, whether by life or by death.—Philippians 1:20

As we live, we can positively sideswipe others, family members, neighbors, friends, and strangers with the eternity in us. Let us pass on living, hope-filled words of challenge and comfort, and let us be doers of deeds of practical kindness, understanding, and love while we are in this life. Today and tomorrow and the next day.

Being sideswiped by eternity helps me notice and appreciate the hidden beauty in other people, even those who are very different from me, from many backgrounds and cultural and religious traditions. Being sideswiped by eternity helps us reach out to others, actively pursuing them down roads of deeper understanding and appreciation of their dreams and aspirations as contributions to my enrichment.

We see eternity in action in the horrors of the World Trade Center bombing and during Paul's imprisonment. But we must, for ourselves, ponder the questions for all religious people, but especially for the church of Jesus Christ: Do we sideswipe others with the Christ within us even in times of difficulty, even when we ourselves are afflicted and burdened with cares and worries? Do we give comfort to others? Is there enough God in us to share with somebody? Can the adverse days through which we currently pass be opportunities to lift the name, life, and example of our Lord and Savior before the world?

Are we like Esther of old, called into the world for such a troubled time as this? Could this be our opportunity to move out boldly in prayer and in appropriate action and response to conditions around us, sharing the peace, love, and prosperity with others in our world?

Paul went about seizing opportunities for Christ. Dare we do less? Let us seize every opportunity to witness for Christ, to sideswipe others with an understanding of his challenge to us in this time of our world's incarceration in the prison house of sadness and desolation.

Paul was on point. He was ready to serve in life or in death, ready. We see his counterparts in so many heroes of the tragedies this nation faced recently. Seizing opportunities.

But let's leave Paul for a minute. If we are to seize opportunities to be a witness for Christ, is it not time for us to ask some serious questions about our own personal journeys? Isn't it time to question our habits and behavior, our individual personality traits and our peculiarities? Yes, isn't it time to look at some of the quirks in us that impede our Christian witnessing power, leaving us chained unproductively to old habits, perpetuating unhealthy attitudes amongst those around us?

Let's make it personal. Why do I let other people get to me and steal my joy and stifle the image of eternity God placed in my soul? Why do I let them keep me from sideswiping them with the eternity and goodness in me?

Let me speak to you about buttons. We all have buttons, you know. If you push the right one, we're sweet and happy and life is good. But if you push our wrong button, we're sour, unhappy, distraught, and life is in the pits. Doesn't it sometimes seem we're at the mercy of all the button pushers around us? Do you know there are some people who just enjoy going around pushing the wrong buttons in your life? Husbands and wives can be wrong button-pushers and enjoy doing it. They know exactly how to create all sorts of havoc for you when they want to.

We sometimes go to great lengths to dodge our button pushers. We even try to avoid our partners if they are pushing the wrong buttons on a given day. It is harder to do at work, but some people do seclude themselves to avoid interaction with coworkers who push their wrong buttons all the time.

The apostle Paul said we should not put away but overcome with the gospel all the negative button pushers in our lives. Sideswipe these people with eternity, with the immortality in you. Disconnect the button pusher with the help of the love of Jesus and the power of the Holy Spirit. Disconnect the negative button pusher with your eternity.

Do some people frequently push your anger button? Disconnect it! Get more Christ in you. Manifest the eternal in you, and you'll shame the negative out of them. Overcome evil with good. Stop allowing people and events to control your life. Put all the buttons under your own control, under the control of the eternal in you. Sideswipe the wrong button pushers with the eternal God in you right now!

Take an inventory of your life. Disconnect altogether those things that do you more harm than good. Seize the opportunity to sideswipe them with eternal goodness and love and understanding.

Paul writes to the Philippians: "For I live in eager expectation and hope that I will never do anything that will cause me to be ashamed of myself. But that I will always be ready to speak out boldly for Christ." Paul's hope is that he never will be shamed into silence. He looks away from shame and toward Jesus Christ. Cowardice might make him keep silent when he should have spoken. Paul is certain that in Christ he will find courage never to be ashamed of the gospel and that through Christ his labors will be effective for all people to see and acknowledge Christ in him, the hope of glory.

Paul's expectation is that he will be given boldness of speech in times of crisis. To speak the truth with boldness is not only the privilege of the servant of Christ, it is also at all times his or her duty. So if Paul courageously and effectively seizes this opportunity, the result will be that Christ will be glorified in him. It does not matter how things go with Paul—whether he lives or dies. If he dies, his will be the martyr's crown. If he lives, his will be the privilege still to preach and witness for Christ.

This is the terrible responsibility of the Christian. Once we have chosen Christ, once we have become members of his church, by our life and by our conduct we bring either glory or shame to Christ. A leader is always judged by his followers, and Christ is judged by us. Run with Jesus until your weight becomes your wings.

*Preached September 30, 2001*

# *Emergency Room Religion*

> And Gideon said unto him, O my Lord, if the Lord be with us, why then is all this befallen us?
>
> —Judges 6:13 KJV

Come with me as we focus on the ancient question asked by Gideon, judge of Israel. It is a question with ageless applicability. Isn't it the question we ask as we face one crisis after another? Why, God?

Isn't Gideon asking, If God is for us, why are so many things going against us? Life is like that for us. We are sometimes bombarded by so many challenges that we can't wait to make an appointment with God for next Monday. We need him right now!

For many of us, as for the Hebrews in the time of Gideon's judgeship, our times call for emergency room help. We have probably all experienced times in our lives when our health was in jeopardy and we anxiously sped to the emergency room of the nearest hospital for immediate help. We felt our problems were both life-threatening and overwhelming. We didn't care who was on duty in the emergency room. We just needed a doctor, someone to see us and take care of us NOW! In the emergency room the medical personnel realize they are dealing with life-and-death situations, so they move with dispatch. They move swiftly to save lives.

Sometimes we face situations when we think God seems to move too slowly, when he seems to be slow in coming to our aid. This is the time for 9-1-1—emergency room religion. Have you noticed that there are no atheists in the emergency room? Everybody there is calling on the name of the Lord, even if they don't follow his ways or practice his precepts anywhere else. I have never known anyone who, facing a crisis, refused a prayer for God's help and healing in their time of need.

Now, what is emergency room religion? Let's put it this way. Some people trust God in theory with ease. They are convinced there is a divine creator, responsible for the existence of this wonderful world in which we live. And how reassuring to be told that he is a loving heavenly father. . . . All this is very good.

But when our lives are suddenly thrown into a state of collapse, when we are broken by the accidents of existence, when our horizon is rimmed about with enemies, then trust in God is no longer a theoretical problem for us. Trust becomes a very practical problem, and we need to come to grips with it. For many Christians their faith does not furnish help in emergencies, so we ask in our desperation, "Will God get to me before it is too late?" Will God get to us before it is too late?

Now enters Gideon, and he comes to the emergency room of heaven and asks this question (Judg. 6:13 KJV): "Oh, my Lord, if the LORD be with us, why then is all this befallen us?" He presses on, "And where be all his miracles which our fathers told us of, saying, Did not the LORD bring us up from Egypt? but now the LORD hath forsaken us, and delivered us into the hands of the Midianites."

Gideon, son of Joash, judge of Israel, presents this emergency need to the Lord. But first, a little background. From his earliest beginning, Gideon and all of the Hebrew people had heard marvelous stories of God's miraculous dealings with the Hebrews. How he brought their forefathers out of Egyptian bondage. How enemies who blocked their way were subdued. How strongholds were taken without a blow being struck.

Gideon, along with many other Hebrews living during those times, believed these wonderful stories, no matter how incredible or improbable they seemed. But at the same time, Gideon felt that victories of the past were meaningless if God could not help them with the problems of the present, if God could not subdue the enemies with whom they were currently dealing. Emergency room religion answers this question: how can we depend on God to help us in the time of urgent and present need?

And what was their present need? Why were they having trouble? A prophet, speaking to Gideon, gives reason for trouble: "But ye have not obeyed my voice" (Judg. 6:10 KJV).

What an appropriately descriptive statement, for our times as well. Is this not the reason for many of our tribulations? We, too, have failed to obey the voice of God. And in sharp contrast and juxtaposition, Judges 6 points to the faithfulness of God to the people he led out of Egypt. But he went further. As they ventured deeper into the Promised Land, they knew him as the God who drove their enemies from them, who fought their battles for them. All they were required to do was be true to him, to have no other gods before him.

But the Hebrews adapted too easily to the surrounding culture and fertility religion of the Canaanites they had recently conquered with God's help. How quickly and easily they forgot their promise to God to be true to him. Here they are backsliding for the third time since the death of Joshua, successor to Moses. God had kept his part of the bargain. For, with his help, they had defeated King Jabin of Canaan, along with his nine hundred chariots. You would have thought they had learned the lesson that, without God, they were weak as water. You would have thought they would bind themselves into a tribal confederacy of faith, suppress Baal and Astarte worship by stringent laws and turn their hearts completely to God, who saved them over and over again from disaster and defeat. But this did not happen. In fact, it would be another one hundred years before they truly repented, for their true reformation leader had not yet been born.

Now, Deborah had been the judge immediately before Gideon, and we read of her good work in Judges 5. She passed through the land, administering justice and commanding the destruction of heathen altars. For a while the people heard her and shouted in loud affirmation that Jehovah is their God and king. But the tide of pious living lasted only twenty years, and in the time of Gideon the people backslid again.

After the death of Joshua, there were no Hebrews left on earth who had been part of the exodus from Egypt. All of that first crowd of Hebrews had died. Could that be the reason they backslid? No firsthand knowledge of God's great deliverance from Egypt? I don't think this is valid justification for their apostasy.

So let's look closely at what was transpiring among the Hebrews during the time of Gideon's judgeship. The Hebrew settlers had begun serious work in the fields and towns. They were breaking new ground, building houses, repairing roads, and organizing traffic. But they were also falling into their old habits of friendly interaction with the Canaanites. Look at them talking to their pagan neighbors near the borders of their vineyards and wheat fields about the prospects of their crops. Slowly but surely they joined the Canaanites in their festivals of the new moon and harvest.

And in their own cities, some of the Hebrew farmers sacrificed to Baal and gathered about Asherim. Though a few earnest Hebrews were indignant in the face of this idolatry, the masses of the people were so taken by their own prosperity they couldn't be aroused to oppose what seemed to bring them success in this new land. For it seemed that peace and comfort on earth were better to them than contending for anything in heaven.

There arose in the center of Palestine a coalition of Hebrew and Canaanite cities with Shechem as their head. These consolidated cities recognized Baal as their patron and worshiped him as the master of their league. And the northern tribes were no better. They had very scant knowledge of Jehovah and could see no great task he had given them to do.

This apostasy is the reason some of the Hebrews rushed to the emergency room. Justifiably, the Lord had delivered them into the hands of their enemies, the Midianites. But after seven years, the Lord appeared to Gideon (Judg. 6:12 KJV): "The angel of the LORD appeared unto him and said unto him, The LORD is with thee, thou mighty man of valour. And Gideon said unto him, Oh, my Lord, if the LORD be with us, why then is all this befallen us?"

This was the Hebrews' blind spot, an example of their flawed reasoning. They felt if they lived and multiplied and inherited the land, they had fulfilled their function as God's nation, as God's people. They could see no great task given to them beyond their own creature comfort. And this is a temptation common to all of us. We convert our own existence and success into a Divine End and think that this is all God requires of us. And it follows that we hold on to faith in God partially because of our desire to have him provide for our own happiness, to make our lives more comfortable.

Yes, the year was filled with seasonal occupations during Gideon's time. When labor in the field was over, there were houses and cities to enlarge, to improve and furnish with means of safety and enjoyment. One task, no more than completed, suggested another to these new Hebrew settlers. Industry took on new forms and taxed the energies of the people even more. Education, art, science, all became possible and in turn made their demands on their time and energy and devotion.

But all they were doing was for themselves, as all we are doing when we go to the emergency room is for ourselves.

God was merely, and still is for many, the great patron who, we feel, should be satisfied with our tithes—when that's all we give him. And we expect attention twenty-four hours a day, seven days a week.

Let me give a contemporary example of the way our nation is moving. Observe the way people are living and the struggle they face to warm their bread and keep a roof over their heads.

Robert Bellah, professor of sociology at the University of California at Berkeley, writing on the discrepancies throughout history between the haves and have-nots, has rightly observed that the masses always did the low-skilled work for which they needed no education or even motivation. Rather, the need was that they be controlled. With the rise of nation states and developments in early and rudimentary warfare technology, wars could not be fought by aristocrats; they required an infantry that was able to understand that rudimentary technology. In addition, with the industrial revolution of the seventeenth century, a huge labor force became necessary to work in factories. The modern welfare state was built, since societies required the active and skilled participation of the masses in the army and the factories, and they had to be rewarded with something.

But here is our problem today: with the new technology, most people are just no longer needed. Not needed in the army, where technological sophistication, not masses of infantry, is seen as the key to success. Not needed in the factory where computers and robots have replaced workers on the assembly line. In short, labor is devalued and most people today are just not needed for anything except minimum wage service jobs.

The problem for the elite becomes, again, how to control the masses, not how to include them: control them with television as long as possible and with police and prisons when that doesn't work.

The critical Christian question, the emergency room religion question, is this: how do we share the enormous productivity of the new economy with those who are no longer required by it? Not much more than one hundred years ago about 70–80 percent of Americans were on the farm; now only 3 percent are required for farm labor, and the percentage is steadily dropping. Fifty years ago, somewhat fewer than 45 percent of all Americans were employed in manufacturing, but today only 16 percent are, and the numbers are decreasing daily. *Emergency room situation*, I would think. The remaining 80 percent comprises the vast category of service workers largely underpaid and marginal. The average wage for males is thirty thousand dollars and for females is twenty-two thousand dollars. Bellah concludes our economy doesn't need many jobs, at least many well-paying jobs, though that is where the wealth is. But our society badly needs certain jobs. We pay more to parking attendants who watch our cars than to people who watch our children. Only massive transfers of wealth from the economy to the society will seriously confront the job crisis that exists in all advanced industrial societies.

We are in the emergency room because the impulses and hopes of faith are made to minister to egoism and selfishness.

But this is far from acceptable to God. For though worship be refined and elaborate, though great temples be built and thronged, though art and music be employed in raising devotion to its highest pitch . . . still, if nothing beyond myself is seen as the aim of existence, if national Christianity realizes no duty to the world outside, religion decays and we need to quickly take ourselves to the emergency room. We as a people can be truly religious only with the missionary spirit. That spirit must constantly shape individual and collective life.

Having no sense of a common purpose great enough to demand their unity, the Hebrews were again unable to resist their enemies, and the Midianites seized their opportunity. God will always get us when we neglect our duty. Let a person neglect his fields, and nature is upon him with weeds choking his crops; his harvest is diminished, and poverty comes to him like an armed man. So in our lives though we subdue the Canaanites one day, the next, other foes are not far away.

Prayer is your 9-1-1—your emergency room religion. Some criticize prayer, calling it egoistic, but we know the heavenly is the only hope of the earthly. That we understand God is not the chief thing, but does he know us? Is he there above, beside us forever? For us, is there a sense of neglect of duty, a sense of disobedience, of faults committed?

First, know that evil now seen may be remedied.

Second, forgiveness is implied in this hope, and it will become assured as the hope grows strong.

Third, the mistake is often made of supposing that an answer to prayer does not come until peace is found. In reality, the answer begins when the will is bent toward a better life, though that change may be accompanied by the deepest sorrow and self-humiliation. The person who earnestly reproaches himself for despising and disobeying God has already received the grace of the redeeming spirit.

Prayer is your 9-1-1: your Emergency Room Religion.

*Preached September 29, 1996*

# Part 2
## *Finding Our Path*

We have become a self-centered, individual-centric, isolated society. We are largely concerned with taking care of our own basic needs—food, shelter, security. And we have very little energy or time left to devote to those around us. We interact with devices as much as, if not more than, we do people. We bemoan and yet celebrate our 24/7 lives and all the urgencies intrinsic to that tempo of existence. People who put in eighty hours a week at the office are held in honor, but with all this comes a myopic tunnel vision.

The rest of the world drops away, and all we can see is ourselves and the very narrow perspective in front of us. Some of us feel we are locked in a solitary struggle for survival. Others of us defy God, wondering, Why do I really need God if I'm able to provide for all my needs? We have lost our path. Instead we are on a precarious course. We focus on, What are my needs? How do I please myself? I. Me. Us.

We have no time for walking across the street to chat with our neighbor. We make no time, nor do we have any trust for meeting strangers. But despite the many artifices we acquire to bolster our independent lives, we simply cannot do it alone.

And all the prescriptions and tonics and therapies in the world cannot save us from our cycle of frenzy, despair, and loneliness.

Our challenge is how to live both individualistically and as communitarians.

The church plays a prime role in bridging this gap. It is the connector that pulls us all out of our caves of self-imposed hibernation and immerses us back into the compassionate arms of community. Community keeps our philanthropic role as stewards at the forefront as it reminds us to take care of that which is not ours, and in so doing we find peace and fulfillment. We find peace when we contribute, when we find our path with God, when we grow from a self-focus to an other-focus. We do not find peace in our solitary despair. We do not find peace or rest until we share with others who we are and what we have! What we have, in the first place, is not ours. It's a gift.

Through our extended Ebenezer family and through our service outreach programs, we continue to create a church community of generosity. In the process we move from a mentality of scarcity to a theology of abundance.

Ebenezer is committed to staying in the inner city and doing community programs in our neighborhood. We are not running off to the suburbs. We are developing community within our community first, and then branching out. Ninety-five percent of the services we provide are not for members of our congregation but are for those on our streets. We are already providing for fundamental needs like food, clothing, employment counseling, and adult day care, and those offerings will be expanded with the completion of the MLK Sr. Community Service and Educational Building.

Martin Luther King Jr. did the global work. We have to come up with the local action. Ebenezer Baptist Church cannot be a monument only, but has to be an instrument. Heroes and monuments offer little unless they galvanize others to act, to contribute. Martin was an activist, and we have to be instruments to continue what he started.

In these messages, we discover that we are often unaware of the unique individual gifts we possess. They could extricate us from many of the personal and societal difficulties we face. We don't know ourselves! Once our personal God-given gifts are identified, we can move from islands of selfishness to share these gifts with others on the mainland. . . . Together we can overcome.

We as individuals and citizens of this wealthy nation might well examine and scrutinize a few of the self-deceptions that are by-products of our affluence. Then let us stand close to King David and confess our guilt. Conversion and sanctification are slow processes. We have to work at both every day. It is not easy to be "washed thoroughly from our iniquities, and cleansed from our sin." But when this process begins, through God's grace, we may lead transgressors to paths of reconciliation and peace.

Finally, if we want personal assurances that we shall overcome, such guarantees are available. We cannot intellectually "know God," but this is his assurance to us. He knows us thoroughly and still loves us, in spite of us! This is sufficient.

# *Lose Your Ticket?*

> Once Jesus was asked by the Pharisees when the kingdom of God was coming, and he answered, "The kingdom of God is not coming with things that can be observed; nor will they say, 'Look, here it is!' or 'There it is!' For, in fact, the kingdom of God is among you."
>
> —Luke 17:20–21

Robert Fulghum writes about being in the Hong Kong airport in 1984 and seeing a young American traveler weeping. After waiting in the airport for two days for her flight, she'd just discovered that she'd lost her ticket. Well, that was almost more than she could bear. She'd been sitting in that one seat for over three hours, and she was desperate. Fulghum and a couple from Chicago offered to buy her lunch and talk to the airline about her problem.

So she stood up to go with them to lunch, smiling with tired relief and turned around to pick up her belongings from her seat. Then she screamed. It was her ticket. She'd found her ticket. She had been sitting on it for three hours.

Did you lose your ticket? Do you know you could be sitting on it? Do you find yourself in despair, depressed and stranded? Could it be possible that you are your own worst enemy? Are we sitting on the power of God that can get us to the kingdom of heaven . . . that can really get you home?

Let's finish the story. How did it end for the girl at the Hong Kong airport? "Like a sinner saved from the very jaws of hell, the young woman laughed and cried and hugged us all, and then she was suddenly gone. And we never saw her again. Off to catch a plane for home and what next."[21]

Often we have been sitting on our own tickets, sitting on whatever it is that will get us up and on to what comes next in life. Fulghum ends his essay by speaking these words to the young woman from America he never has seen since that day: "Thanks, you have become, in a special way, my travel agent. May you find all your tickets and arrive wherever it is you want to go, now and always."[22]

Did you lose your ticket or are you sitting on it? Well, let's apply this to our lives and ask three questions.

First, are we sitting on our ability to be kind and hospitable, or have we lost our tickets? Paul brings this squarely before us by asking, are we living by the spirit or by the flesh? Listen to his instructive words:

> Now the works of the flesh are obvious: fornication, impurity, licentiousness, idolatry, sorcery, enmities, strife, jealousy, anger, quarrels, dissentions, factions, envy, drunkenness, carousing, and things like these. I am warning you, as I warned you before: those who do such things will not inherit the kingdom of God. By contrast, the fruit of the Spirit is love, joy, peace, patience, kindness, generosity, faithfulness, gentleness, and self control. There is no law against such things. (Gal. 5:19–23)

But haven't we lost the ticket to the kingdom of kindness, generosity, faithfulness, gentleness, and self-control? We need to turn from hostility to hospitality. That's what Robert Fulghum and the people in the passenger lounge did in Hong Kong as they ministered to the need of that young, lost woman who couldn't find her ticket. And it doesn't take a lot of people to move a home, an airport, a place of employment, or even our cities from arenas of hostility to hospitality.

Let us illustrate. A recent Gallup poll says that if you are looking for human kindness and hospitality you have a better chance of finding it in Rochester, New York. Gallup measured acts of kindness in thirty-six cities, rating the top city in giving, helping, and caring as Rochester and the lowest, the erstwhile city of brotherly love, Philadelphia.

Why are some cities hostile and alien? The high density of population, the way urban people are crowded together may be the fundamental seedbed of urban rudeness, which falls harder on strangers than anybody else. Too many people living in tight places often leads to short fuses in human relations.

However, this is not the complete answer. Several cities with much less dense populations than those in our eastern corridor are also rated poorly in hospitality and openness to help a stranger.

I was impressed with the fact that the city of Rochester was ranked number one in 1941, as well as in 1994. Why was it number one fifty years ago? Because of the tradition of giving started by George Eastman Kodak, who gave money and created services in that city for many years. Giving to charities indicates what kind of heart the city has. Have we lost our ticket to the kingdom of hospitableness? Are we locked in hostility? It only takes a few who give to turn it around.

The kingdom of God is among you. It is within you. But have you lost your ticket? Where in your life is there evidence of the fruit of the spirit in you? Where is love, joy, peace, patience, kindness, generosity, faithfulness, gentleness, and self-control? You have to follow the law, but there is no law against helping those who have lost their tickets in life.

The second question is, How do we lose our ticket to life in Christ? By being brain dead or heart dead? Medical science teaches that for all practical purposes we are medically dead when we are brain dead. That's a hard concept for us to assimilate, for even after a patient is brain dead they can be hooked to a ventilator. The chest rises and falls, the skin color remains good because capillaries are kept filled with oxygen-rich blood, so that the patient who is brain dead merely appears to be sleeping peacefully.

But in Christ we are more concerned about being heart dead. Your brain may be alive, but if your heart is dead is that not worse? Even though we know intellectually that a person's ability to feel, care, love, and hate is not really centered in the heart, we still speak of heartache, of being heartsick. We ask heartless, uncaring people to have a heart. We ask hopeless people to take heart. We yearn for heartwarming stories. So it is really difficult for the Christian to accept death, spiritual death, as anything other than an uncaring heart.

Third, did you lose your ticket to your close relationships with the person you say you love? Let me put it another way: Which is more important to you—your work or your marriage or the person you love? Naturally most people will say, "My loving relationships are more important than my work." Yet if I ask where you spend most of your prime time, chances are you would say, "at work." One knows work is necessary, but in the process have we lost our tickets to wholesome and loving relationships? Let's just look at the facts. At our places of employment, the people we interact with usually get the best of us, so to speak. We do our best to be polite and attentive to all of the people we interact with. But by the time we come home to the most important persons in our lives, our families, we neither have the energy nor patience to be polite and attentive. So when we get home or around those we love, we dispense with tact, diplomacy, courtesy, and other graces, telling ourselves, at least at home or in the company of the person or persons I love, I can be myself.

But allow me to ask one simple question. Why do so many of us think that being one's self almost never implies being one's best self? Why is it that when we let it all hang out we are often rude, insensitive, noncommunicative, unkind, uncaring? Why do so many of us believe that being oneself almost never means being our best self with the people we say really count? If we love them, why are they getting the short end of the stick, the crumbs that fall from the table? Have we lost our tickets in the areas of our love commitments to those who are our own family members or dearest friends?

The physician Luke wrote the deeds of the early apostles. At times it seemed as if the early church had lost its ticket, forgotten why it was sent into the world. Over and over again he had to remind the early Christians facing persecution and serious suffering that the kingdom of God is not coming with things that can be observed; nor would they say, "Look, here it is!" or "There it is!" For, in fact, the kingdom of God is among you—within you.

The book of Acts, which Luke penned, tells us of the history of the church over about thirty-two years after the death of Christ. And it may well surprise a thoughtful reader to note how little progress Christianity seems to have made at the end of that thirty-two years, so far as the outward life of humanity is concerned.

For nothing amounting to great social change is recorded here. In thirty-two years the kingdom of God had not put down heathen sacrifice nor demolished a single idol temple. Scarcely did people's public and social life show any traces of the kingdom of God. In looking down upon the crowded dwellings of the great cities of the Roman Empire, you would not have seen the spire of one church. For three hundred years there were no buildings which gave note to the great moral revolution that had taken place through Jesus Christ.

And yet, though you couldn't see it, the gospel was indeed then fermenting with peculiar power in the hearts and minds of women and men. The kingdom of God was at the very center of their inner life.

The mustard seed had been cast into the earth, and it was swelling and bursting beneath the soil. The leaven had been thrown into human nature, and its influence, though noiseless and unseen, was subtly and extensively diffusing itself throughout the whole lump. Christ's religion was to win its way noiselessly, like himself.

"Do not be afraid, little flock, it is your Father's good pleasure to give you the kingdom" (Luke 12:32).

God wants you to find your ticket. It is within and among you. May you find all your tickets and arrive wherever it is you want to go, now and always.

*Preached August 21, 1994*

# *Healthy, Wealthy, and Wise?*

> Because thou sayest, I am rich, and increased with goods, and have need of nothing; and knowest not that thou art wretched, and miserable, and poor, and blind, and naked:
>
> I counsel thee to buy of me gold tried in the fire, that thou mayest be rich; and white raiment, that thou mayest be clothed, and that the shame of thy nakedness do not appear; and anoint thine eyes with eyesalve, that thou mayest see. As many as I love, I rebuke and chasten: be zealous therefore, and repent.
>
> (Revelation 3:17–19 KJV)

Today we visit John on the island of Patmos, and we delve into the revelation John received there.

There were seven churches to which God gave a message through John the Revelator. We focus on the seventh church, the one at Laodicea. Listen to John's words in Revelation 3:14–16:

> "And to the angel of the church in Laodicea write: The words of the Amen, the faithful and true witness, the origin of God's creation: I know your works; you are neither cold nor hot. I wish that you were either cold or hot. So, because you are lukewarm, and neither cold nor hot, I am about to spit you out of my mouth."

What a devastating message sent to the church at Laodicea. Listen to the way John greets the six other churches and note the obvious contrast.

To the church at Ephesus he writes: "I know your works, your toil, and your patient endurance."

To the church at Smyrna: "I know your affliction and your poverty even though you are rich."

To the church at Pergamum: "I know where you are living, where Satan's throne is, yet you are holding fast to my name, and you did not deny your faith in me."

To the church at Thyatira: "I know your works, your love, faith, service, and patient endurance."

To the church at Sardis: "I know your works. You have a name of being alive but you are dead. Yet you have still a few persons in Sardis who have not soiled their clothes. They will walk with me dressed in white for they are worthy."

To the church at Philadelphia: "I know that you have but little power and yet you have kept my word and have not denied my name."

But when we come to the church at Laodicea, the risen Christ has absolutely nothing positive to say.

Why no commendation for the church at Laodicea? Why only admonition and correction? The church at Laodicea certainly had a positive view of itself. It thought of itself as a healthy, wealthy, and wise community of believers. But John saw them differently as he assessed their progress on the Christian way.

What made Laodicea think of itself as an important city in ancient times? The city had four claims to fame. First, its location. Laodicea was nestled on the great main road east of Ephesus on the way to Syria. It served as a major commercial center for the many travelers who had to pass through it on the way to Syria or back to Ephesus. Originally, it was a small town. But after the Pax Romana it grew not only in commerce but as a great banking and financial center of the ancient world.

Second, Laodicea had wealth. You could cash big checks in this city. It had numerous financial institutions to serve the mammoth crowds coming through the region. In fact, history records that when Cicero was traveling through Asia Minor he would always go to Laodicea to cash his letters of credit. The banks could handle the emperor's financial needs at Laodicea, for it was one of the wealthiest cities in the world. When an earthquake devastated it, the citizens of Laodicea refused help from the Roman government. No, they were independent. From their own resources they rebuilt their city.

No wonder they could brag about their wealth. They needed nothing materially. In fact, they were so wealthy, at times they wondered if they really needed God.

Third, Laodicea was wise. It used its wealth and resources wisely, and as a result its wealth grew. The Laodiceans were fortunate because the city was a textile center. The sheep that grazed around Laodicea were famous for their soft, violet-black wool, and the Laodiceans mass-produced and exported outer garments, cloaks, capes, and tunics. They had clothing outlets, primitive but the precursors of our Burlington Coat Factories.

But now to the fourth gift, the one that made Laodicea outstanding: health. Probably the most important gift of all is health. There was a medical school in Laodicea, and it was world-famous for two medical ointments: one for the ears and one for the eyes. The eye salve was shipped, in fact, all over.

Yet John declares the Laodicians had healed eyes but couldn't see, and restored ears but couldn't hear.

In light of the city's wealth, wisdom, and health, why is the writer John so displeased with the Laodiceans? This church was made up of people who were rich and had good savings and investments. It was a city with a large surplus in its treasury, and its economy was doing extremely well. Therefore it felt that it needed no outside resources of any kind. Who worries about being right with God when everything around us is going on quite well without him? Laodicea never realized that it was naked in the sight of God. They were so wealthy they didn't think they needed God. So well-clothed they didn't see they were nude before God.

Because they were rich they thought they only needed to be ceremonially Christian. But here comes John with some disturbing news for all of us: Who are you trying to fool, he seems to be asking.

We think we are healthy, wealthy, and wise without God? Look at the other side of the story. The church in Laodicea suffered from an attitude of indifference. Of all things in life, indifference is the hardest to combat. It is said that an author can write a good biography if he loves his subject or if he hates his subject, but never if he is indifferent to his subject.

If you have been convicted by Christ, you can't be indifferent. Indifference can only be broken down by the actual demonstration in our lives that Christ is the power making our lives strong and the grace making our lives beautiful. The problem of modern evangelism is not hostility to Christianity but indifference.

*You can't be indifferent about that saving act of God in Christ Jesus. It saved you and me.*

The Christians at Laodicea tried to be neutral, but being neutral to Jesus is impossible. For to be neutral to Jesus is to be an obstacle to Jesus. You see, Jesus works through people, and when we remain completely detached and neutral, we in essence refuse to undertake the work which is the divine purpose for us. Therefore, we are not on the way, but in the way.

What does it take to break the cycle of hopelessness in the world today? We can't be neutral about it. Indifference. Neutrality. Followers with reservations. God cannot use us when our loyalty may turn into indifference.

> *I counsel thee to buy of me gold tried in the fire, that thou mayest be rich; and white raiment, that thou mayest be clothed, and that the shame of they nakedness do not appear; and anoint thine eyes with eyesalve that thou mayest see.*
>
> *As many as I love I rebuke and chasten. Be zealous therefore and repent.*
>
> *Behold I stand at the door and knock: if any man hear my voice and open the door, I will come in to him and will sup with him, and he with me.*

The risen Christ advises the Laodiceans to buy gold tried and refined in the fire. Get faith that has been tried in the fire. The Laodiceans were wealthy, but wealth cannot buy happiness. Wealth cannot give us health either of body or mind. Wealth cannot bring comfort in sorrow nor fellowship in loneliness,

But if we have a faith that has been tried and refined in the crucible of suffering, then there is nothing that we cannot face. We are wealthy indeed. And if all we have is what we meet life with materially, we are poor indeed.

In the ancient world, being stripped naked was the worst shame and humiliation one could bear. On the other hand, to be clothed in fine raiment was the greatest honor. Clothes don't make the man or the woman. No clothes in the world will beautify a person whose nature is twisted and whose character is ugly.

Healthy, wealthy, and wise. Who are we trying to fool?

Dr. George MacDonald, the old Scottish divine, is helpful as we end:

> Come to me Lord I will not speculate how
> Nor think at which door I would have thee appear
> Nor put off calling till my floor be swept
> But cry, come Lord come anyway, come now
> Doors windows I throw wide, my head I bow
> And sit like some one who so long has slept
> That he knows nothing till his life draws near.[23]

*Preached September 14, 1998*

# *Please Wash Me!*

> Wash me thoroughly from mine iniquity, and cleanse me from my sin. . . . Then will I teach transgressors thy ways; and sinners shall be converted unto thee.
>
> —Psalm 51:2, 13 KJV

Have you observed how very often on a dirty truck, car, or bus, someone will trace three words in the surface dust: "Please Wash Me!"

Robert Fulghum writes that he loves washing things. In fact, he is in charge of doing the laundry for his whole family each week. Now, I don't know how his car looks, but washing clothes gives him a sense of accomplishment. It represents his involvement with his family, and it gives him time to reflect about some deep matters.

But one day his washing machine and dryer both died, and he had to go to the laundromat. As the laundry went round and round in the washer and dryer he recalled how we once believed disease was an act of God—until we figured out that it was a product of human ignorance. We've been cleaning up our act, literally, ever since. We've been trying to get the dirt, the waste off our hands and clothes and bodies and food and houses and cars and trucks and buses from time immemorial.

Then Fulghum hits us with his most profound observation. If only scientific experts could come up with something to get the dirt out of our minds, lift the grime from our lives, soften our hardness, protect our inner parts, improve our processing of life, reduce our yellowing and wrinkling and improve our natural color and make us sweet and good.[24]

Please wash me.

Well, once upon a time, David the king and psalmist asked God to do just that for him. Please wash me, O God. He lifts up his lamentation in his plea sung in his fifty-first hymn of Israel. "Have mercy on me, O God, according to your steadfast love; according to your abundant mercy blot out my transgressions. Wash me thoroughly from my iniquity, and cleanse me from my sin" (Ps. 51:1–3).

Here we find King David in one of the lowest valleys in his life. He has been caught and denounced for a terrible crime. Nathan, the prophet, has exposed him for taking Uriah's wife, impregnating her, having Uriah killed, and then after his death, taking her as his wife.

It's open to interpretation, but I hear in these words the personal confessions of sin from a broken and contrite king, longing for cleansing, burdened by consciousness of sin and by the realization of his awful solitude and separation from his God. It is amazing that David still felt he had a chance with God. So he goes to the tent where the ark is and asks to be washed. Nathan told David that God had not deserted him, but there were conditions to be met and sufferings he would have to endure, so the king still prayed to God hoping that the prophet was right.

"David said to Nathan, 'I have sinned against the LORD.' Nathan said to David, 'Now the LORD has put away your sin; you shall not die. Nevertheless, because by this deed you have utterly scorned the Lord, the child that is born to you shall die'" (2 Sam. 12:13–14).

You will not die but you will lose something. This is the ground of David's plea. The revelation of God's love for him precedes and causes true penitence. And for us as well: "Have mercy on me, O God, according to your steadfast love, according to your abundant mercy blot out my transgressions."

What do we need God to wash out in us? By his steadfast love and abundant mercy . . . this is our detergent. Let us look carefully at our sins. Sin is seen as transgressions, iniquity, and missing the mark. Blot out my transgressions. Blot out my rebellions. Sin is also rebellion. Religious rebellion is the uprising of my will against the rightful authority of God.

But we need to be careful to observe that these rebellions, these transgressions, are not merely the breach of abstract propriety or law, but opposition to a living person, to the living God who has the legitimate right to be obeyed by us.

The definition of virtue is obedience to God. Sin is the assertion of independence from and opposition to God. Conceive of the washing, of cleansing, as forgiveness.

Our past is a blurred manuscript, full of flaws and typos. And we despair, believing what has been written can never be changed. But the psalmist and the prophet knew better. Though foul legends of false gods may have been written on the scrolls of our past, devotional meditations may be written by a saint, obliterating our bad writing. God's lore can be written there, blotting out our past rebellions, still partially visible.

But let us move on to verse two: "Wash me thoroughly from my iniquity." If transgressions are our rebellions needing to be blotted out, what does the word "iniquity" mean here? Iniquity is that which is twisted or bent. Wash me thoroughly from my twisted and bent life, my distorted life.

There is a straight line to which our lives should run parallel; our life's paths should turn aside for nothing but go straight to their aim over mountain and ravine, stream or desert. But this man David's passions made for him a crooked path. He was involved in twisted and bent living, in the same wandering mazes that get us nowhere.

That's where God finds many of us, caught up in twisted and bent-up, banged-up, distorted, out-of-shape relationships. You and I need to be washed thoroughly from them. Unravel my twisted and bent living. Almighty God, please wash me as you did David.

We pray for the spirit. Create in me a clean heart, and put a new and right spirit within me. Do not cast me away from your presence, and do not take your holy spirit from me.

Restore the joy of salvation and sustain in us a willing spirit.

*Preached August 6, 1995*

# *We Can't Know, but We Can Be*

> If I speak in the tongues of mortals and of angels, but do not have love, I am a noisy gong or a clanging cymbal. . . . For we know only in part, and we prophesy only in part; but when the complete comes, the partial will come to an end. . . . For now we see in a mirror, dimly, but then will will see face to face. Now I know only in part; then I will know fully, even as I have been fully known.
>
> —1 Corinthians 13:1, 9–10, 12

Let me begin with this statement: too often, people judge themselves by what they do rather than by what they are.

Allow me to tackle the problem of knowing ourselves, for truly this is one of the most difficult tasks we have in life. We cannot really know ourselves. We are mysteries to ourselves. And the truth of our mystery is itself a mystery. The more you try to fathom yourself, the more fathomless you are revealed to be. You can't understand yourself. I cannot understand myself.

For no matter how much of yourself you are able to objectify and examine, the quintessential living part of yourself conducting the examination will always elude and escape you.

So I am sorry to disappoint you, but I doubt that you will ever solve the mystery of yourself. All you can do is just live out the mystery in you. For you see, we solve the mystery of self not by fully knowing ourselves but by striving to fully live out being ourselves. So breathe a sigh of relief. You can't know you, but you can still be you!

I will deal with the knowledge of God and self: we can't know but we can be—but I must first say a word about love. The thirteenth chapter of 1 Corinthians is Paul's exquisite word on love as the hallmark of our Christian journey. Paul says God's love is the most expensive and qualitatively endowed gift of all the gifts of the spirit.

Philosopher Martin Buber defined theology as "talking about God" and religion as "experiencing God." We need less theology and more religion, more opportunities to find moments in our lives when we feel we just met God.

Among us are many gifts of knowledge: learning; eloquence; sagacity; musical, poetic, and artistic genius; business acumen. And yet they often reside in people who seem to carry no evidence of personal religion. They have begun a Christian career, but they might be deteriorating in character instead of developing and maturing.

Love is the ligament that attaches, that binds together the several members of the body of Christ. Love is the cement that keeps the stones of the temple together. Without love there can be no body, no temple, only isolated stones or disconnected and therefore useless members of the body of Christ. No other gifts can compete with love. Other gifts may profit the church, but without love, there is no evidence of Christian growth into mature Christian personhood.

Listen to Paul as he explodes the myth that mere knowledge about God is sufficient. "If I speak in the tongues of mortals and of angels, but do not have love, I am a noisy gong or a clanging cymbal" (1 Cor. 13:1). John Bunyan also suggests that we may do wonderful works in Christ's name and still be rejected by him because no love undergirds our efforts.

As Paul also notes in 1 Corinthians 13, knowledge of ourselves is fleeting. We call this knowledge the backbone of character. Well, this too shall pass, it shall be no more. Knowledge, even of ourselves, won't stand the test of time and circumstances. God is a mystery, but it is the knowledge of God and divine things in which good people delight.

Paul helps us understand this by using the image of an object dimly seen through a semi-transparent medium, a glass darkly (or a mirror dimly). When we speak of imperfect knowledge, we mean one of two things: we mean that it is imperfect in amount or imperfect in quality and accuracy. When we learn a first principle we can add to it, but we can never improve on that principle. Our knowledge is imperfect in amount, but so far as it goes, it is absolutely reliable. We may build upon it and deduce other truths from it. But let's face it, in this life, we only know in part. We are always becoming. We can't know the things really essential for us to know. We only know ourselves in part.

Take the problem of being angry. Some of you can focus on this right away. Are you angry at somebody at this moment? Picture them. I bet you can bring them right up on the screen of instant recall. What do you *know* about your anger?

Paul said anger is to be expected, but don't let the sun go down on your anger. Anger is an emotion with which most of us struggle. Moses had a short fuse. Jesus could be angry. He cleansed the money changers from his father's house. We know we don't need to hold anger inside ourselves, for we know that anger repressed or denied will never be eliminated.

In fact, the longer you hold on to your anger, the more destructive its effects become in your life. What are the results of anger? Depression, impatience, a critical attitude, sleeplessness, physical ailments, and even ulcers.

So what can you do about it? Evaluate your anger. Ask yourself some questions. Be as honest as you can with yourself. Here are four questions I want you to ask about your anger:

1. What is really making me angry?
2. Why do I feel anger and not some other emotion?
3. Am I overreacting to this situation?
4. Am I angry because I'm not getting my way?

Practice forgiveness today. Don't let the sun go down. When your anger is directed toward someone, ask God for power to forgive that person. When anger is directed toward yourself for some mistake you made, forgive yourself. Forgiveness is a great remedy in overcoming anger. Don't let anger rule. And don't say that's just the way you are, and that you can't change.

Author Bruce Barton put it well when he wrote, "When you're through changing, you're through."[25]

But back to knowing, this seeing through a glass darkly. What does knowing in part mean?

When we walk on a misty morning and see an object up the road in the distance, our knowledge of that is imperfect in the sense of being dim, uncertain, and inaccurate. We say, there is something before me, but whether it is a human being or a gatepost, I cannot tell. I know only in part. As I draw closer I see it is a human being, but whether old or young, friend or foe, I cannot say. But my knowledge is moving from dimness to accuracy.

Our knowledge of godly things is like this: godly things loom in the mist. Many of their details are invisible to us. We can't understand them.

We have not got them under our hand to examine at leisure. Our present knowledge is as the light of a lantern by which we pick our way, or as the starlight for which we are thankful, but we pray for the morning and the rising sun when truer, more full knowledge will be available to us so that partial knowledge shall be eclipsed.

In this life, we know only the general outline of unseen reality. But hereafter we shall know even as we are known. We shall not have the same perfect knowledge of him that he has of us, but we shall see him immediately and directly as he sees us.

We do not know, but we can be because he knows and sees us.

*Preached March 3, 1996*

# Part 3
## *Finding Meaning in Our Lives*

Never have we been so overstimulated, overwhelmed, and overburdened as we are with today's high financial, moral, and spiritual price tags. How do we live generously with others and yet remain responsible to ourselves? How do we share each other's burdens? We say there's a value in that, but we don't really do it. How do we walk the walk? How do we put God first?

Kids today, encouraged by TV and video games, believe you solve problems by zapping. Answers and resolutions are supposed to be instant. Evident. No thinking or reasoning or faith necessary.

But we know answers are not instant in coming and sometimes not even apparent. What we do know is that the key to meaningful living cannot be possessed. It's what you give . . . of yourself, of your love. And that the real treasure in this world is not gold or silver . . . but love, from God and from the people in your life. Do good. Be rich in good deeds.

What we often mistake as real problems are really mere inconveniences. And the pleasures that accompany honor and wealth pay far fewer dividends than faith.

Sometimes we need to step off the merry-go-round, exit from the superhighway, be silent. To reflect, pray, meditate. To commune with nature or God or our spirit. Think of it as a portable Sabbath, available anytime. In quieting our harried heads and hearts, we find meaning and balance.

In these messages, we confess that we really don't want to be bothered with the problems of others. We're too preoccupied with our own. And to get ahead, we are quite willing to sacrifice respect, integrity, honor, community, and God (if the price is right), regardless of the harm done to others (e.g., WorldCom and Enron).

We are motivated by an egotistic, selfish "need-theology," which has little room for self-denial and cross-bearing. Is this the reason life seems to have little meaning? Is this the reason we feel empty? How shall we overcome? Perhaps it can happen as we rediscover meaningful relationships with family, friends, and nature. Perhaps we might best take time to enjoy each other and life.

Judas Iscariot was also searching for meaning, personal significance, political ascendancy, and relief from oppression. But for Judas it had to come through wealth and fame, yet he really wanted so much more. . . . He is a complex figure. I just can't figure him out!

# *Profit or Loss? (Part 1)*

Robert Fulghum tells of a well-to-do, self-satisfied man who left his house one morning with a cup of coffee and his briefcase, as normal, climbed into his Range Rover, and began to drive to work. He ignored the continuing honking of a neighborhood woman from the Episcopal church, and of Fulghum himself, who both followed him, but eventually was so frustrated that he slammed on his brakes, ready for a confrontation, only to watch his expensive leather briefcase and his coffee slide off the roof of his car and onto the ground. Fulghum writes:

> Now he's not a bad guy. . . . I think he may not know as much as he needs to know about the most basic business concern of all: profit and loss. Here's a very old profit and loss statement to put on the wall of my business and maybe of yours as well. It's a business statement from the lips of Jesus himself. It is a lesson to be learned by all of us. "What does it profit a man or woman to gain the whole world and lose his own soul, his own life?"[26]

What will a person give in exchange for his soul, his life? How does your balance sheet look this morning? Profit or loss?

Are you harassed, driven, getting nowhere, spilling your coffee, forgetting your briefcase, ruining your day, running on a full gas tank and an empty soul? Look at your life as I view mine. Is it a profitable existence, or are we really suffering great losses in many areas of our existence? Go to the mirror. Profit or loss? The question to the man in the Range Rover is a question that Jesus could address to each of us. Where do we place our values in our lives? Could our values be on the wrong things?

In Fulghum's story, the man in the Range Rover couldn't appreciate his neighbor's help because he was not sensitive to the depth of his own problem, the seriousness of his own plight. Many of us don't comprehend how much trouble we are in until it's too late to do anything about it: when our coffee cup is smashed and our briefcase is run over.

But congratulations to the people who tried to warn him of the impending loss he was about to bring on himself. The woman went out of her way to help. She was not reluctant or embarrassed to try to save him. Be witnesses. For Jesus said, "Those who are ashamed of me and of my words in this adulterous and sinful generation, of them the Son of Man will also be ashamed when he comes in the glory of his Father with the holy angels" (Mark 8:38).

And he makes this promise to the faithful: When the king comes into his kingdom he will be loyal to those who have been loyal to him, faithful to those who have been faithful to him, kept their promises to him, rain or shine.

Yes, this is an adulterous and sinful generation, but be faithful and you will gain the profit given by God himself.

No person can dodge the trouble of some great undertaking and then reap all the benefits of it. You reap what you sow. You can't refuse service in some campaign and then share in the decorations when the campaign is brought to a victorious conclusion.

When we are tempted to prefer an easy and prosperous life, rather than a fruitful but stern and even perilous course, then we are in danger of becoming not the mouthpiece of Jesus but the mouthpiece of Satan, the evil one. What shall it be, this life of yours and mine, in the profit or loss column?

To all of us, Jesus says, danger and hardness are not to be chosen for their own sake, but to reject a noble vocation because they are in the way is to heed not the voice of God but the whims of society and culture and Satan.

In Mark 8:34, Jesus calls the people together and gives his inflexible law to us all: Every follower must deny themselves, take up their crosses, and follow him.

The angry man's irritability is due to remorse and self-reproach, for a deeper hidden evil, gnawing away at his soul. And he knows it. That's why he is bitter.

Profit or loss. How do we lose as individuals?

First, we may sacrifice honor for profit. Some of us desire material things and are not too particular about the way we get them. Our world is full of temptations toward profitable dishonesty. We are little thieves: "They won't miss this silverware," we say. It's a high-class restaurant, and we want some class.

Second, we may sacrifice principle for popularity. We need to remember that it is not the verdict of public opinion but the verdict of God that settles destiny.

Third, we may sacrifice lasting things for cheap things. Many a thing or activity is pleasant for the moment but ruinous in the long run.

How can we balance our books? By reality testing: the test of eternity, the test of seeking to see the things as God sees them, is the great reality test of all. A person who sees things as God sees them will never spend his life on the things that lose his soul, his life. We can sum it all up by saying a person may sacrifice eternity for the moment of pleasure. We would be saved from all kinds of mistakes if we always take the long heavenly view.

We've looked at ourselves. Let's look now at our family time. What does it profit a family to gain the whole world and lose its soul? In the face of competing demands by coaches, school instructors, youth religious instructors, and other activity leaders, family activities like dinners, weekend outings, vacations, and visits to relatives are the first priorities to go.

How can we reclaim that time? Here are a few tips:

- Assess your schedule and ask if it allows you enough time for what's most important. If not, examine why. Is it sheer lack of hours or misspent time watching TV or playing video games? Is it parents' work schedules or children's activity commitments?
- Keep a log of how many times your family eats or spends time together. It will shock a partner who is reluctant to give up his or her activities.
- Make accommodations so everyone can eat dinner together.
- Keep the TV off during dinner and out of your children's rooms. Both discourage family conversation and interaction.
- Don't underestimate the importance of bedtime routines and rituals.
- The key words to reclaiming family time: keep it simple and consistent.

Profit or loss?

When writer Anne Lamott defended her practice of making her fourteen-year-old son go to church, even though he hates it, she was bombarded by critics who accused her of child abuse and brainwashing. But Lamott suggests that since we live in confusing times, a little spiritual guidance never hurts any of us.

Doing uncomfortable things is weight training for life. Anne Lamott knows God also loves teenagers who don't go to church, but such teens are deprived of seeing people who love God back. Learning to love back is the hardest part of being alive.

Lamott also makes her son go to the church youth group, because children want people who will sit with them and talk to them about the big questions of life.

It would do us well to examine where our values lie. Profit or loss?

*Preached September 7, 2003*

# *Profit or Loss (Part 2)*

## Fearing and Blushing

> Those who are ashamed of me and of my words in this adulterous and sinful generation, of them the Son of Man will also be ashamed when he comes in the glory of his Father with the holy angels.
>
> —Mark 8:38

Remember the lady who tried to help her neighbor in Robert Fulghum's story? She was not ashamed of her Christian faith, nor afraid to reach out in helpfulness to her neighbor, even if he was rude and ungrateful. She was not afraid to get involved. She was not afraid to witness. She blew her horn to warn her neighbor that he was about to lose something valuable. Yes, her witness was positive. She was a soldier of the cross. She did not fear to own his cause . . . or blush to speak his name.

Let us think about this topic: fearing and blushing.

The question found in the Scripture passage for today is this: Was the apostle Peter embarrassed by Jesus, ashamed of Jesus? Are we embarrassed by him as well? Did Peter fear to own Christ's cause or blush to speak his name?

The scene is at Caesarea Philippi. Peter has declared, when asked, that he believed Jesus was the Messiah, the son of the living God, the soon-to-be-victorious deliverer of his people from cruel centuries of oppression. But then Jesus jars Peter by not speaking of victory but of defeat. He tells of this impending crucifixion at the hands of his enemies. And the disciples were embarrassed. They were suddenly ashamed to hear Jesus utter these self-defeating words because the idea of a suffering Messiah was utterly foreign to the expectations of Israel.

This announcement was keenly painful to Peter. Hadn't Jesus promised to build his new church upon this affirmation that he was the mighty Messiah, the son of God? Hadn't Jesus promised his apostles and the church the keys to the kingdom of heaven? Power. Such power. What they bound on earth would be bound in heaven, what they loosed on earth would be loosed in heaven? And now this! What a disappointment, what a shock, what an embarrassment. This was so far away from their dreams, and especially Peter's dreams for the future. He never envisioned he would embark upon a career defending a losing savior and supporting a lost cause even before it started. Peter just didn't want to be partner to a persecuted, martyred Messiah.

Quite to the contrary, in fact. He was intoxicated by prospects of the great position into which he was suddenly thrust. You remember the words of Jesus: You are Peter, and upon this rock I will build my church.

Peter was feeling his oats. He allowed himself this strange freedom of attempting to interfere with Christ's plan. Yes, he took Jesus aside and began to rebuke him. But Jesus in turn rebukes Peter, telling him that his sentiments for his protection were in reality stumbling blocks in the way of his messianic mission. Jesus warned Peter that he had misunderstood the purpose of his Lord.

"Peter, you've got to be prepared to die. To bear a cross, as I will."

Do we fear to own his cause or blush to speak his name?

Fearing to own his cause. But no person can dodge the trouble of some great undertaking and then reap all its benefits.

Now, we try to transform small difficulties into large crosses. Sometimes we don't even know the difference between an inconvenience and a problem. If you break your neck, if you have nothing to eat, if your house is on fire, then you've got a problem. Everything else is an inconvenience. Life is inconvenient. Life is lumpy. And a lump in the oatmeal, a lump in the throat, and a lump in the breast are not the same. Learn to separate the inconveniences from the real problems.

Do you fear to own his cause and blush to speak his name?

Peter did. He said he would die with Christ, never forsake him. But when he was standing around the fire that night he denied even knowing Jesus. He would not speak his name. It made Peter blush to speak his name.

We blush when we pray at restaurants. Some people deem it prudent to conceal their relationships with Jesus Christ, for if we are to live successfully in this world, the worldly wise encourage us to hide our faith. We must be in outward compliance with the customs of our time, so we don't show any outward evidence of faith in God. We think you only need internal invisible evidence of a heart that is right with God.

It is also declared by some that if it is necessary to make a show of my faith, I exhibit it at the peril of my own life and comfort. Doesn't God seem to be an insensitive and unnecessarily difficult master? These are really just excuses on our part as we attempt to justify shunning the arduous challenges of gospel obedience. They illustrate that we are ignorant of our own religion and the great ends to be served by our Christian faith.

If you think there is some inward security that is agreeable in his sight and renders you acceptable to him, you are mistaken. For our attempts to conceal our true motives, our hypocrisy, should make us detestable to God.

The day shall come when the last self-deception shall be at an end. The cross of the Son of Man, that type of all noble sacrifice, shall then be replaced by the glory of his father with his holy angels. He will turn his face from us. What price shall we offer to buy back what we have forfeited?

We do fear to own his cause and blush to speak his name. Remember, you were bought with a price. He paid the ransom after we were kidnapped by sin. Testify to this adulterous and sinful generation what he did for you. Don't give up the faith for honor or wealth or pleasure. That was Peter's mistake.

*Preached September 21, 2003*

# *Judas Iscariot*

## All He Saw Were Pockets (Part 1)

After saying this Jesus was troubled in spirit, and declared, "Very truly, I tell you, one of you will betray me." The disciples looked at one another, uncertain of whom he was speaking.
—John 13:21–22

Today we will attempt to understand a few of the complex motives in the mind of the most despised disciple of Jesus. We focus on Judas Iscariot, who betrayed Jesus, turning him over to his enemies, who took his life by means of a criminal execution, by crucifixion.

And we will ask some penetrating questions about Judas: What strange wheels were rotating in his mind, prompting him to betray the most tender heart ever to beat within a human breast? What maliciousness dominated his soul to the extent that it pushed him into heartless disregard for the prince of peace, the son of God? Isn't this the reason we shun him? Isn't it true that no parent names a son Judas since the time of this unprofitable man? We will examine Judas's motive. What was the driving force that accelerated his almost unpardonable sin?

Let me start with a contemporary story. The Sufis are mystics in the Islamic tradition. Their leaders are famous for sharing profound teaching stories, which are never told as preachments to be obeyed. Quite the contrary. When the Sufis tell their stories, it is left to the hearers to do with them as they may choose, and to take on whatever level of meaning suits them. You are not compelled to be or do anything after hearing the Sufi's story.

An Islamic scholar related this Islamic mystic's story: A famous religious teacher was passing through a small town. It was known that he carried with him the secret key to understanding, the meaning of life. A certain pickpocket approached him, looking for that key to the meaning of life. He searched the teacher with his talented fingers, but found no key and turned away empty-handed. All he felt were pockets.

Could this be the clue to understanding Judas Iscariot? He was one of the handpicked twelve disciples of Jesus Christ, the savior of the world who knew the secret of the meaning of life. But Judas was looking for a key to the secret of life's meaning in something tangible, a key he could hold in his hand and claim as his own and put in his bank account. So he searched Jesus with his talented fingers for three years, found little or nothing, and turned away from him, empty-handed, bitter, and withdrawn. Why? Because all Judas saw were pockets.

And maybe we are not that far from Judas. For don't we have to admit that often it is our pockets, our possessions that are of utmost importance to us? Too often, we think of them as the key to the meaning of our lives.

But let us go to our biblical passage as we try to understand Judas: "After saying this Jesus was troubled in spirit, and declared, 'Very truly, I tell you, one of you will betray me.' The disciples looked at one another, uncertain of whom he was speaking."

Now the first question that leaps to the curious mind is this: what troubled Jesus? Well, he has reason to be troubled for he is only a few hours away from Calvary. But biblical insight makes crystal clear that Jesus was troubled, because one of his trusted disciples and alleged friends, Judas Iscariot, treasurer of the band, was going to betray him, sell him out to his enemies who wished to eliminate him, to kill him.

Notice, Jesus isn't surprised that he was to be betrayed, though it wounded him deeply and added immensely to his grief to know it was one of his familiars who would do this. A friend would do this.

But he knew it would happen even before it actually occurred.

Now, isn't it amazing that Jesus not only eats with Judas but also washes his feet, as he did with all of the other disciples? Jesus never recompensed evil for evil. He seeks always to overcome evil with good. But why the foot washing?

On the way to dinner at the Pharisee's house that Wednesday evening the Twelve were engaged in a deep and fiery argument about their future positions and importance in the kingdom Jesus described. Who would be the greatest among them? they wondered out loud. Who would have the most prominent position?

Their quarreling became so heated that the disciples were almost out of control when they arrived at the Pharisee's home. They entered the home of their host no longer talking with each other. They didn't even look across the dining space at each other. So what did Jesus do? "[Jesus] got up from the table, took off his outer robe, and tied a towel around himself. Then he poured water into a basin and began to wash his disciples' feet and to wipe them with the towel that was tied around him" (John 13:4–5).

The disciples are now totally ashamed of themselves, of their pettiness regarding position and prestige, of their unwillingness to serve each other or anybody in humility and in love. Jesus, their master, gave them this example of true grateful servanthood as he took care of the dirty but needful work of the kingdom.

And he washed Judas's feet also, even though Jesus knew of his planned betrayal. Judas was still Jesus' friend, so far as the Lord was concerned. That's what hurt Jesus so much . . . when friends, not enemies, betrayed him.

But what were Jesus' purposes in washing his disciples' feet? What he intended was not merely to wash the soil from their feet but to wash from their hearts the hard, proud feelings that were so uncongenial. He wanted to wash away thoughts that so threatened his cause and his kingdom of peace and love. We need to be washed.

Jesus points out that all who were washed were not cleansed. They may have been clean on the outside, but something evil and sinister was brewing on the inside. For their feet did not need cleansing as much as their affections and esteem for one another did. They needed wisdom to understand that humility and love are the greatest forces for change in our world. Jesus was trying to demonstrate this to his disciples. After the foot washing, the feet of Judas were as clean as those of John or Peter, but Judas's heart was foul.

Now Jesus could have easily eaten with people who were unwashed but not with people who hated one another; who glared fiercely and hostilely across the dining table at one another; who declined to pass dishes they were asked for to one another; who displayed silent, cold malice and bitterness of spirit.

By washing his disciples' feet, Jesus displayed deep humility and love. And the disciples there that evening were not proud of their conduct; they all wanted to trade places with Jesus and wash his feet and their fellow disciples' feet, for they finally understood the kind of kingdom he was inaugurating. All would have traded places with Jesus—except Judas. It became crystal clear to Judas that he was in the wrong mix and needed another kind of savior. On that night, Judas came to the sad realization that the kingdom about which Jesus spoke would not be one of conquest, wealth, position, and prominence. He would have nothing to show the world that he had gained by being Christ's disciple for three years. Nothing in his hands. Nothing in his pockets. And all he could see were pockets. For this kingdom Christ described was spiritual, not material. It wasn't about pockets. It was an internal state of mind and soul. It wasn't quantifiable.

So he pulled away, moving in the opposite direction from Jesus. He began to calculate ways to cut his losses in their religious enterprise. *How can I get something out of these three years of following Jesus all around this land*, he wondered? How can I save myself from the embarrassment of this empty, lost cause so frowned upon by the religious and political authorities? Well, if I can just break up Jesus' movement quickly, quietly, and suddenly, I'll be justified in my disgust with Jesus while at the same time counted a useful servant of the religious and secular authorities of my day.

So the idea gradually crystallized in Judas's mind that the best use he could make of Jesus would be to betray him, to sell him to his enemies for all the money he could acquire for doing so. For all Judas could see were pockets. Empty pockets at that.

Now, a traitor is always treacherous. Never forget this! And it is most difficult to forgive treachery. Why is this so? It is because a treacherous person uses knowledge against you that only a trusted friend could have. He uses it against you to betray you to your enemies. A treacherous person divulges intimate confidential information you thought he would never expose because he knew it would harm you, causing pain and suffering to you or your family and dearest friends. You needed somebody to talk to, and you trusted him. A very treacherous person can often be a dear friend, even a family member, a fellow church member.

If Jesus had unmasked Judas's treachery to the rest of the disciples at supper that night, Judas wouldn't have gotten out of that dining room alive. But this is not our Lord's way of dealing with treacherous friends.

Why did he wash Judas's feet? Our Lord hadn't given up on Judas, not yet. He was still trying to convert him, even in his final hour. Jesus did his uttermost to win Judas's heart and loyalty but to no avail. It was just no use.

But we are forced to ask, "Why did Jesus choose Judas in the first place to be one of the twelve disciples?"

Our Lord knew Judas to be a man of low repute, a man who was not remorseful or repentant for past wrongs. He knew that Judas, especially at this time in his ministry, was out of harmony with the other disciples. Furthermore, Jesus knew that Judas was a false friend, plotting to save himself by bringing ruin on Jesus and the rest of the disciples. Jesus knew that Judas was cold and callous.

Why then did Jesus still patiently bear with Judas? Because Jesus does not mistake present defilement for habitual impurity, nor partial stain for total uncleanness. He does not suppose that because we have sinned this morning we have no real grace in us.

Back to the mystic Sufi and the pickpocket, who saw only pockets. Does Jesus want me to be poor? Judas wondered about this out loud, and so do we. How are we to live as middle-class Christians in a needy world? Some twenty-five years ago, Ron Sider, in his book *Rich Christians in an Age of Hunger*, first introduced evangelical social action. He asked, Can a Christian be a disciple of Christ without becoming poor? Can a person continue in a middle- or upper-class lifestyle and still be living as God desires? Do we have to be poor to follow Christ? Absolutely not, Sider answers.

The biblical perspective is for us to live in wholeness, which includes a generous sufficiency of things. Poverty is a bad thing. God wants us to have all we need for a joyous life. God wants no one poor. But poor in spirit is a deficit far costlier than poor in pocket.

*Preached September 22, 2002*

# *Judas Iscariot*

## All He Saw Were Pockets (Part 2)

> One of his disciples—the one whom Jesus loved—was reclining next to him; Simon Peter therefore motioned to him to ask Jesus of whom he was speaking. So while reclining next to Jesus he asked him, "Lord, who is it?" Jesus answered, "It is the one to whom I give this piece of bread when I have dipped it in the dish." So when he had dipped the piece of bread, he gave it to Judas son of Simon Iscariot. After he received the piece of bread, Satan entered into him [Judas]. Jesus said to him, "Do quickly what you are going to do."
>
> —John 13:23–27

It was utterly impossible for Jesus not to be deeply disturbed and anxious as he ate from the same dish as the disciple he knew had already betrayed him, sold him out to those who hated him.

Eating from the same dish was an act of friendship, fellowship, and companionship. When you eat from the same dish you trust the persons with whom you are eating. But Judas can no longer be considered a friend nor true disciple. He was no longer in this category. His treachery needed to be exposed for what it was. His hypocrisy needed to be revealed for what it was. Treachery hurts more because I trusted you. I confided in you. But notice our Lord does not name his betrayer in this account. Nevertheless, he singles him out and sends him from the table to complete this most despicable mission by a process no other disciple could comprehend. Jesus still protects Judas, for no one at the table knew why he said to Judas, "Do quickly what you are going to do."

Some probably surmised that since Judas had the common purse, Jesus was telling him to buy what they needed for the festival. Or that he should give something to the poor. "So, after receiving the piece of bread, he immediately went out. And it was night" (John 13:28–30).

There were three things our Lord did indicate, however, about his betrayal. Number one is: Among my disciples, there is a traitor. In utter bewilderment they looked at one another, unable to detect guilt in the faces of any of their companions. Nor could they recall circumstances in the past that would make them suspicious of any in their number.

"Master, is it I?" they asked. At all costs they must be cleared of this charge of betrayal. And the question, "Is it I, master?" expresses the deep pain and piercing shame they felt. For the very thought of being false to Jesus wounded them intensely. But there was one of them who didn't join in asking, "Master, is it I?" For Judas knew.

The second thing Jesus indicated was the process of indicating the betrayal. "One of his disciples—the one whom Jesus loved—was reclining next to him; Simon Peter therefore motioned to him to ask Jesus of whom he was speaking. So while reclining next to Jesus he asked him, "Lord, who is it?" Jesus answered, "It is the one to whom I give this piece of bread when I have dipped it in the dish" (John 13:23–24).

Look at Judas. Suddenly he ceases dipping anything into the bowl, for he knew the noose of suspicion was tightening around his neck. Jesus offers him the dish, but Judas refuses to take it. And the look of Jesus at Judas that accompanied his refusal shows that Jesus knows Judas is the betrayer. He has been discovered by this process. Eating with the enemy in the inner circle.

The third indication of betrayal is when the Lord says to Judas, "Do quickly what you are going to do." Only John and Jesus know the meaning of Judas's abrupt departure from the dining room that night. And John perceives that Jesus wishes Judas to leave unobserved and undetected. So as difficult as it was for him to restrain himself, he follows the desires of his Lord. He doesn't scream and point his finger at Judas and say, "He's the one, grab him, stop him!"

And though Judas need fear no violence at the hands of John, this disciple's writing later clearly exposes Judas for what he was.

He writes, "He went immediately out; and it was night." It was night. Yes, it was night in far more ways than one.

Now as we delve more deeply into Judas's character and personality, trying to understand why he betrayed the Lord, we are forced to declare that Judas was a mixed man, a complicated man; in fact, Judas might be called a double-minded man. But I hear you say, So what's new? A lot of us have complex personalities. Some of us qualify as double-minded individuals, too.

OK, but let's look at Judas's personality with a little more discerning scrutiny. Judas had, on the one hand, an extraordinary capacity for wickedness, but, on the other, an inclination toward that which is good. We start with the positive in him. That's always the place to start if we truly want to understand anybody—friend or foe.

Our Lord initially saw in Judas gifts and abilities that would make him extremely useful to him in his saving purposes for the world. And likewise, Judas was very impressed with Jesus initially—so impressed that he was willing to give up his profession to follow him. He, like Peter and the other disciples, boasted about what he had given up to follow Jesus.

Judas may have followed Jesus hoping to receive honor, position, and wealth in this new kingdom Jesus was on the verge of inaugurating. And we know Judas was trusted by Jesus and his disciples, for they allowed him to hold the common purse, to be custodian over their funds. They thought they could turn their backs on him and he would be honest. Notice, the purse was not entrusted to the beloved disciple John, for he was too much a dreamer for practical affairs. Nor was it entrusted to Peter, for he was too impulsive and they would have soon been in great financial difficulty. Nor even to Matthew who knew financial affairs. But to Judas Iscariot. Judas was best at wise financial decisions. He was good at watching over the pockets of their common treasury. Certainly they thought him a man of character and integrity, or they would never have selected him as their treasurer.

But there is another good characteristic about Judas that we need to lift up. He was a man with an active conscience. How can I say Judas had an active conscience when he betrayed Jesus for thirty pieces of silver? I can say it because after the betrayal of our Lord, Judas is overwhelmed with an acute sense of shame and remorse for what he had done.

In fact, his sense of guilt is stronger even than his love of money, which had before this been his strongest passion, his deepest motivation for living. And in his final act, suicide, we can find a reason for respecting Judas; he doesn't try to get off the hook. He judges himself fairly and sees what he has become by betraying Jesus and willingly but sorrowfully goes to his own place. He recognizes that his proper habitation is hell and hangs himself and goes there.

Let's not get confused. Judas is still a man of mixed motives. A complicated man. A double-minded man. For despite all of his assets—his good impulses, his resolute will, his enlightened conscience, his frequent feelings of affection toward Jesus, and his desire to serve him—he committed a crime so unparalleled in wickedness that men make little attempt to compare it with sins of their own. To betray the son of God for something to put in his pockets is the worst thing he could do.

Let's go deeper. Why did this good man with mixed motives go off the deep end? What drove him over the edge?

It was Palm Sunday that destroyed Judas, that pushed him beyond reason. Maybe beyond sanity. You see, Jesus had come into the city in triumph on Palm Sunday, but he seemed indisposed to make use of his popularity to make some big money on this his biggest day. A marketing opportunity. "This is your chance, Jesus," shouted Judas. "Take up the collection. Get the tithes and offerings today. It's Palm Sunday."

And when Jesus didn't capitalize on this golden opportunity Judas was utterly disgusted with Jesus. He was through with him now and forever.

Why did he betray Jesus? Some have alleged that Judas was tired of Jesus missing opportunities for prosperity and material riches. So he thought he would bring the matter to a boiling point by giving Jesus over into the hands of his enemies, hereby forcing him to reveal his true power to save himself. After all, isn't self-preservation the first law of nature? Don't all of us look out for ourselves first and foremost in this world? But it's more than this. Why did he follow Jesus in the first place?

I believe Judas not only wanted to follow Jesus to get into his kingdom for money but also to rid himself of a major character flaw within himself: covetousness. Judas wanted to be with Jesus so he could fight his weaker covetous nature. We are all double-minded, and our minds often contradict our values. Judas was a covetous man, and he needed to rid himself of his covetousness, his greed, his grasping. He was in with Jesus for the wrong reasons, however. And then Judas shifts gears and moves into exceptional wickedness. After Judas received the gift of God from Jesus himself, Satan entered into him. Exceptional wickedness surrounded by the most blessed goodness in the world. Satan and Savior on the same stage? Jesus' sorrow is similar to that of the psalmist: "It was not an enemy that reproached me; then I could have borne it. . . . But it was thou, a man mine equal, my guide, and mine acquaintance" (Ps. 55:12 KJV).

It was the treachery that made our Lord's betrayal so unbearable. It was the wicked work of Satan using Judas as a tool of his own to effect a purpose that never should have occurred . . . the betrayal of God's only son and our only savior.

Exceptional wickedness. Now, this sin was not the natural product of Judas's human heart or a heart like our own. Rather, it was the demonic work of Satan, prodding our Lord's friend and disciple to turn against him, the best friend Judas and the others had ever had. He would give up anything to save Judas, and yet Judas betrayed him. When Satan gets you, you lose all scruples. Judas had none now.

This was his problem: the garden where Jesus prayed was not sacred to Judas. Judas preferred to use Jesus in a little moneymaking scheme for his own good. For all he saw were pockets. After Palm Sunday Judas's self-restraint was breaking down. His covetousness was getting the better of him. And so, sadly and regrettably, but with bitterness, Judas felt he had to break away from Jesus and his friends, the other disciples.

The sin of Judas teaches us the great power and danger of the love of money. Yet it was not the thirty pieces of silver but

Judas's embitterment and desperation that moved him so negatively. He had allowed money to become his all. All he could see were pockets.

And he was a disappointed man. The other disciples, finding the kingdom of Christ to be spiritual, were pure and high-minded enough to see that their disappointment was their greatest gain. The love of Christ had transformed them and to be like Jesus was enough for them, but Judas still clung to the idea of earthly grandeur and wealth. When he found Christ was not going to get him these, he became sour and embittered.

For the danger of this passion is here. It is the failing of a sordid nature, this love of pockets. It is a little, mean, earthly nature. The love of money is also dangerous because it can be so easily gratified. All that we do in this world, daily, is in most cases connected with money.

Judas had his fingers on the bag all day. It was under his pillow at night. He dreamed about money as the secret key to all things good and beautiful. But he thought of this as his privatized sin. Every covetous person fancies this is something that is his own business and will not damage his religious profession or ruin his soul as some reckless infidelity will.

They retain command of their own life and are prepared to go with Christ only as far as they find it agreeable or inviting. They are seeking to use Christ and are not willing to be used by him.

The result is that they one day find that even through all their religious profession and apparent Christian living, sin has actually been gaining strength. And finding this, they turn to Christ with disappointment and rage in their hearts because they come to see they have lost both this world and the next. They have lost many pleasures they might have enjoyed, and yet have gained no spiritual attainment.

But the comprehensive lesson that this sin of Judas brings with it is the rapidity of sin's growth and the enormous proportions it attains. And to discover the wickedness of human beings, to see the utmost of human guilt, we must look not among the heathen but among those who know God. Not among the profligate, dissolute, abandoned classes of society, but among the apostles.

The good that was in Judas led him to join Christ and kept him with Christ for some years. But the devil of covetousness who was cast out for a while returned and brought with him seven devils worse than himself.

Here is the final word: Jesus held his peace. He demonstrated the more excellent way. He forgave Judas and let him go his way out into the night. Jesus glorifies God by showing that it is better to forgive, even Judas.

As Jesus did with Judas, in letting go, we make peace and stop the cycle of harm. Forgive someone you are angry with today. Forgive yourself. Don't let the sun go down on your anger.

*Preached in two parts, September 29, 2002,*
*and October 13, 2002*

# Part 4
## *Finding Faith*

Faith—the central touchstone in religion.

Faith is the reliance on the divine presence of God. It is the evidence of things not seen. Faith is the ultimate trust that it will work out because we trust God for who he is.

Our assurance is in the truth of the resurrection. The undeserved, unjustified pain and torture that Jesus endured was hell and worse. But that gives us hope. Through Jesus Christ our savior, God has removed our braces, not physically but spiritually. We will die the first death, but he has saved us from the second. We can deal with the sufferings of the present moment and know that we will be united with God. We experience faith when we surrender ourselves to Jesus Christ. We stumble and fumble our way, but through it all, we believe.

And sometimes that's all we can do. We tie a knot at the end of the rope and just hang there and know that God has voted for us.

Now, God does give us freedoms. God is not a puppet master. He does not predetermine our choices. Horrible tragedies befall us, and we implore, "Where was God?" We would not be honored as humans if we were merely puppets. Of course there is free will on earth.

But there is also grace. Grace is the serendipitous entrance of God into moments of our lives when we cannot see how we will make it, but he comes with the divine favor and the comfort of the Holy Spirit.

The closer we get to death, the more clearly we see God. My very rational plans I have seen to be superseded by unmerited favor, and what I thought was smart turns out to be dumb. I have witnessed God working in surprisingly wonderful, unorthodox ways.

Trust, do good, and we'll be fed. Maybe not in the way we expected, but in a way that ultimately transcends our mortal designs.

In all things, God is working for good for those who love the Lord. Things might not be good, but God is good. Grace and faith give us the fortitude to hang in there.

In the following sermons, we seek to discover ways to maintain faith in God. We are often surrounded by circumstances that drive us to despair. The question may be put thusly: How do we personally overcome the harsh realities of the present? Don't present realities negate our trust in the presence and power of God in history? How do the death and resurrection of Jesus Christ provide us assurances that these historical defeats we experience are not ultimate? Can we declare through faith that God still has the whole world in his hands?

In the midst of changing circumstances, how can we find the middle ground between our dreams, on the one hand, and our limitations, on the other? Additionally, can we become selfless enough to transcend our own individual desires, and comprehend our interconnectedness with all our sisters and brothers in the whole world? Through faith in God's trustworthiness in all circumstances of life, can we find other ways to overcome?

We move on to discover how we can face physical death, not relying on our own human capacities, but anchoring ourselves in our trust in God.

Finally, we seek ways to overcome by learning how to deal with worry, and understanding its frustrating origin and futility. Can we surrender ourselves to faithful God, who watches over us and loves us?

# *But You Wouldn't Know It Sometimes*

> The earth is the LORD's, and the fullness thereof; the world, and they that dwell therein.
>
> —Psalm 24:1 KJV

Couple this with the popular spiritual "He's Got the Whole World in His Hands," and we are ready to be introduced to the theologian, poet, and professor Dr. Gerhard Emanuel Frost, who taught for years at the Lutheran Theological Seminary in St. Paul, Minnesota. From one of his writings came the title for this message.

Frost wrote a poetic piece centering on a vexing problem for all of us. It is the problem of certainty, for we are certain of very few things in this life. He speaks about the frustrating difficulty of being certain about anything or anybody:

> It is sermon time in the little chapel of the local retirement home. The sermon carefully prepared and well conceived. The young preacher, holding a globe in his hands, praised the goodness and greatness of God, proclaiming that, "He's got the whole world in his hands." Suddenly from the white-haired sage in the second row, like a blast from a torpedo came this harsh unexpected response. "But you sure would never know it sometimes!"
>
> Enough to sabotage any sermon, but true to the human situation.

> One can't know; one is called to trust. One can never explain one's faith. If it can be explained, it isn't faith. Our certainty is sustained in heaven.[27]

The old man was right. The mystery of suffering can't be solved with certainty in our broken world.

No matter how hard I try, I can't satisfactorily prove either the love or the omnipotence of God beyond the shadow of a doubt.

I would like to be able to meet the puzzling experiences of life with nothing more than simple logic, but at its center, life calls for humility and trust. Above all, living calls for faith. Yes, faith is a vital ingredient in life. Without faith, life becomes boring and fearful. Boring because where there is no faith, there is no hope for a better tomorrow. And fearful because life without faith sees only the worst and anticipates only failure. But you wouldn't know it sometimes.

Faith is the link that bridges the failures in life to the successes. One only goes from failure to better things as he or she travels the way of faith.

Faith is needed if life is to reach the summit and escape the lowlands. Too many settle for the backlands when faith waits to show them the sunrise.

Faith presupposes an attitude of humility, and we don't like being humble, for the world may think it can push us over. We don't cotton to humility. If we are humble, people think we are inferior, subservient.

But the word "humility" comes from the Latin word *humus*, which means rich and fertile soil. Humility is the fertile soil of faith. Like soil, it receives all that God gives. And only then can we sprout upward.

The old man was right. If we insist on proof that God's got the whole world in his hands, then we oversimplify and falsify our lives and our existence. We waste ourselves in anger and hostility toward God. But if we can surrender to his purposes and follow where we cannot see, affirming ultimate meaning without demanding immediate clarity, he will lead us toward the light. And one day we will see. Can we be certain that the earth is the Lord's and everybody in it? Well, that might be true, but you wouldn't know it sometimes. Look at the way they treated Jesus, the son of the most high God, who was innocent, righteous, just, and loving.

Was God in control in Bethlehem when Herod set up a heinous plan to kill all baby boys because he feared that the baby the wise men sought might unseat him someday? Was God in control when Mary and Joseph had to flee with the baby to Egypt, to Africa for safety? Was God in charge? You sure wouldn't know it sometimes.

And to this day we still ask why. Why did the son of God have to die in this manner, by execution set aside for criminals? What did the death of Jesus mean? Why did it have to occur?

To us, physical death is but an appendix to life, a negation, something we would dispense with if we could. But we must pay our debt to nature. A human being, born of woman, will die.

But not so with Jesus. He was born that he might die. Surely then, it was not as a man that Jesus died. He died as the son of God, for men and women of every age, for you and me. To prove that the earth is the Lord's and the fullness thereof. You are God's husbandry. God's product. Made in his image. Distorted, yes, but you are still his.

But what gets me is what happened on the cross. The horror of a great darkness fell upon Jesus' soul. He had borne every torture earthly humans could inflict, without a murmur, until finally he couldn't take it anymore, and he cried out in terrible anguish, "My God, my God, why hast thou forsaken me?"

We can interpret the great horror of his agonizing cry in but one way. The lamb of God was bearing away the sins of the world. He was tasting for us the bitter pains of the second death, and as he drinks the cup of the wrath of God against sin to its bitter end, he feels passing over him the awful loneliness of a soul bereft of God, the chill of the darkness itself. To have broken communication with God the father is worse than anything. When your heart has been broken, was it not because communication was broken?

God is in charge. Well, the old man says, you wouldn't know it sometimes.

In our society you would not know he has the whole world in his hands. There are 34 million Americans living in poverty today. Among them are 7.2 million poor families, 12.1 million poor children, and 12.1 million poverty-stricken elderly citizens, in this, the richest nation in the world.

Jesus lived as our example. He died as our atonement, opening by his blood the highest heaven to us, helping us escape everlasting death. This is our certainty. Our trust in God. This is our faith.

Even when we wouldn't know it sometimes.

*Preached March 7, 2004*

# *Always About to Grasp*

For I have learned to be content with whatever I have. I know what it is to have little, and I know what it is to have plenty.
—Philippians 4:11–12

Father Thomas Merton was a deeply profound, contemporary Roman Catholic mystic. He was also a sensitive social critic. He protested many injustices in our world. A prolific writer, he wrote more than sixty books. But there was a lighter side to the Trappist monk. He found much humor and deep faith in life, but above all, he discovered joy in simple things.

It is reported that he would laugh at theologians who were not happy unless "God was a problem." In his book *Conjectures of a Guilty Bystander* he asked a question that has intrigued me since I first read it: "Why can we not be content with the secret happiness that God offers us, without consulting the rest of the world?"

A very good question. Well worth turning over in our minds, well worth examining carefully. Why can we not be content?

Yes, Father Merton speaks to us about contentment. The blessed apostle Paul does likewise as he writes his Philippian friends while incarcerated in a Roman prison. Listen to Paul's words regarding contentment: "For I have learned to be content with whatever I have. I know what it is to have little, and I know what it is to have plenty" (Phil. 4:11–12).

Well, let's go deeper. Contentment, according to Father Thomas Merton, is that quality which allows us to live fully in the present, seeing the possibilities and the joys at hand, that secret happiness God offers.

Think about it. Isn't it true that so much of our energy and time is channeled into planning future events, future security, and future prospects? Consulting with the rest of the world, as Merton puts it.

Aren't we almost always lining up something for the future? And aren't most of us a little dissatisfied with our present conditions and circumstances? Let's look at a few examples:

Aerobic exercise tapes are sold by the thousands to men and women who are dissatisfied with the shape and condition of their physical bodies. That's alright, but will we ever be content with the way we look? Probably not.

Our car is never quite right. Our apartment is not quite large enough. Our salary is never adequate, and our work is never as fulfilling as we had hoped. Our children aren't as gifted as we had wished. Our spouse is not as romantic as we had dreamed. And our health is not perfect.

We are not content because there are so many places we have not seen, so much delicious food we have never tasted, so many books we have not read, so many classes we have not taken. And time seems to be running out on us, doesn't it?

But know this. If we are fools enough to remain at the mercy of people who want to sell us happiness, it will be utterly impossible for us ever to be content with anything.

For the very last thing a salesman wants the buyer to become is content with what he or she has. How would they profit if we became satisfied or content? You are of no use in our affluent society unless you are always just about to grasp what you never have.

And from this simple thought we derive our sermon title, "Always About to Grasp." Always about to grasp what we will probably never have, what we will probably never possess.

Now, the Greeks were not as smart as we are. In their primitive way, they put Tantalus in hell. In Greek mythology, Tantalus, the son of Zeus, was doomed to hell. As he stood in water wanting a drink, the water receded beyond his reach. When he was hungry and wanted to eat, he could never quite grasp the fruit that hung above his head. He was always about to grasp after the tantalizing object of his desire. Merton says Madison Avenue, on the contrary, would convince us that Tantalus is in heaven.

Our own hell surrounds us when the tantalizing glitter of a materialistic world robs us of the contentment God has to offer us, the secret happiness that can be ours. For you see, God's world is a beautiful world. If we have eyes to see and ears to hear we are doubly blessed.

Contentment? If we have food enough to sustain our bodies for a few days, a place to rest, someone to love, and meaningful work to do, we are richer than the richest person on the earth. God's secret of contentment is for us to become aware of how much we are loved and that God gives us gifts and people who need us.

Now let's get to Paul and the Philippians: "For I have learned to be content with whatever I have. I know what it is to have little, and I know what it is to have plenty" (Phil. 4:11–12).

Now, this is no stoic utterance that we hear from Paul. He was not indifferent to things passing before him. He was very sensitive to the beauty in the present, even while he was in a Roman prison. He was also sensitive and grateful for kindnesses rendered to him, those small acts of the Philippians, those gifts given to him to cheer him up and on while in prison.

But from whence came Paul's confidence and joy in the midst of adversity?

Paul declared that he possessed the joy of the Lord. This joy he had, the world didn't give it to him. The world didn't give it, the world couldn't take it away. This joy in Christ was the rock and anchor of his life: I rejoice in the Lord, he says, that your care for me has flourished again, but if you had given me nothing, I still have the joy of the Lord as the foundation of my faith. My foundation. My secret happiness.

We need to remember that the persons and things around us all have a connection with the Lord, if we have eyes to see and hearts to note this connectedness.

This is true about everything that touches our lives, all persons and things, all occurrences. For all persons and things with which we have to do are in the Lord's world, and the Lord calls us and equips us to deal with them. Some persons are the Lord's servants, but all of them, the Lord calls us to love and to benefit. Even your enemies are connected to God.

So don't worry about grasping after this or that. In fact, as Paul wrote, "Do not worry about anything, but in everything by prayer and supplication with thanksgiving let your requests be made known to God" (Phil. 4:6).

Now, if we do not share Paul's joy, our Christianity will at best be low and comfortless. But when we learn the true rejoicing in the Lord, we will be rewarded by a growing liberty that will free us from a life like Tantalus's, from always grasping for that which we cannot and maybe should not reach.

The more this joy possesses us, the more it will give occasion to the finest and freest play of feeling in reference to passing things, and some of these, while they appear insignificant on the surface, will abound in rich consolation for us.

The Philippians had lacked opportunity to minister to the needs and wants of the blessed apostle. But the wintry feelings, whatever they were, that hindered the expression of their goodwill were over, they were gone, and the Philippians' care of Paul flourished again. Isn't it good to know the winter is over? And isn't it wonderful that the apostle did not think it necessary to freeze up his corresponding feelings of satisfaction toward them, which this prior provocation evoked?

When you are in the Lord, you do not anxiously cast about for help. Paul learned to bring his desires down to the facts of his condition. Have we learned to do this? In this state, he counted on himself to have enough. He knew how to adjust himself to the state of the indigent and friendless, and he knew how to adjust himself to abundance when it was sent. Contentment. In each state, he made himself at home. Not over-grieved or overjoyed, not greatly elevated or greatly depressed. He had been instructed not only into the experience of both of these conditions, but into the way of taking kindly to both of them.

Don't always grasp after things. "Do good and to communicate forget not: for with such sacrifices God is well pleased" (Heb. 13:16 KJV).

Get some passion in your life. Life is not measured by the number of breaths we take, but by the moments that take our breath away.

If you want God's fire to burn brightly in your heart, take out yesterday's ashes.

Finally,

> *There is great gain in godliness combined with contentment; for we brought nothing into the world, so that we can take nothing out of it; but if we have food and clothing, we will be content with these. But those who want to be rich fall into temptation and are trapped by many senseless and harmful desires that plunge people into ruin and destruction. For the love of money is a root of all kinds of evil, and in their eagerness to be rich some have wandered away from the faith and pierced themselves with many pains.*—1 Timothy 6:6–10

*Preached February 29, 2004*

# *Four Ships in a Storm*

> [Jesus] said to them, "Why are you afraid? Have you still no faith?" And they were filled with great awe and said to one another, "Who then is this, that even the wind and the sea obey him?"
>
> —Mark 4:40–41

We remember at the end of the year our loved ones, our sisters and brothers, who were with us but who now are with the Lord. And yet they are with us still, in the corridors of fond and dear memories.

I know your grief is not over. Tears still flow. You glimpse some simple thing in the house that reminds you of them, and the fountains open again and you cry yourself to sleep.

But how grateful they were to all of you who have come to light candles representing your living memories of them. You lovingly gave them endless hours, days, weeks, and in some instances years of personal devotion. You were there for them during the long and restless nights. They were grateful, but sometimes too weak to tell you how grateful they were for your presence, so let me say it for them. Thank you for loving and caring for them. We are grateful, and in a strange way so are you grateful for the privilege of just being there for them. They loved you for it, and God does, too. You will be rewarded. You will see them again.

Our task this day is to help with your healing and ours—to finger the beads of our rosary and to seek to be renewed and restored for our journeys. For you all have miles to go and blessed missions to fulfill.

This morning I want to suggest that there are at least three ways that we respond to the sickness and death of those we love.

Let me begin with a story about four ships in a storm.

The storm blew in, but it was expected. Three sailing ships with cargo from the east were sailing toward Venice, Italy. The captains had been warned that they should anticipate trouble on this voyage, for a storm loomed on the horizon. But when the storm erupted, each captain reacted differently.

The first attempted to sail around the storm, not wanting it to interrupt his voyage. He was in a hurry to get on with his life. He was in denial. The captain of the second ship, unafraid of the tempest, drove his ship straight into the storm. He was macho. "I can take it on."

But the captain of the third vessel ordered that his anchor be put down, for he trusted that the anchor would hold the ship in the middle of the storm.

The tempest broke with tremendous fury, and the first ship was blown hundreds of miles off course. The ship of denial. The second ship was pounded against the shore. The macho man. But the third ship, though nearly destroyed, held firm in its place in the sea.

Our reactions to sickness and death come close to the reactions of these captains in the storm. Let me illustrate this truth with an example taken from a real-life situation.

After two years of struggling with a terminal disease, thirty-year-old Melody died. Her family and friends knew it was coming. They anticipated the storm, but they weren't ready for its magnitude. Some tried to sail around Melody's illness, denying that Melody would die and continuing on as if nothing would happen. But when it did happen, they were blown away, hundreds of miles off course. For in their denial they found no strength to deal with the storm.

A second group of family and friends moved straight into the storm, but having nothing to secure them from its fury they were crushed and pounded against the shore without hope.

But a few cast down their anchor, trusting in God to keep them safe. In the end, these people found peace in her death. Though nearly destroyed, they held on firmly.

Melody herself seized the anchor in the end, and in perfect hope and trust she died a blessed death. All who grounded their anchor in God found safety in Christ in spite of the storm.

Now, these three ships personify three reactions to sickness and death. Does one of them come close to ours? We are all individuals. We react according to our own unique makeup and personal composition.

Let's look more closely at that third ship and its occupants—those who anchored themselves in Jesus, who grounded themselves in God in the middle of the storm.

Johannes Tauler was an extremely popular preacher and mystic, born in thirteenth-century Germany. He lived through the sunset of the Middle Ages and the dawning of the Renaissance, but what I find most significant and helpful for my life in his writings is this: he teaches us to cast our anchor in the ground of the being of God, as seen and known to us in Jesus Christ our savior.

Central to Tauler's sermons was the mystical ideal of becoming one with God. Tauler encouraged his congregation to enter into the ground of the very depths of their own souls. Your soul is the image of God in you. This ground of our soul is where God resides in us, where he can be found in us.

To enter the depth of our souls, through contemplation or by some mystical experience, means becoming one with God. This union with God is a mystical union that can be explained only by experience.

So when you face a storm, listen to Tauler's advice:

> Cast all your anxiety on God! [Be solidly anchored in him.] When sailors are in danger of running aground and all seems to be lost, they throw their anchor overboard and it sinks to the bottom of the Rhine. That is the way they defend themselves against danger. And it is the way we, too, should act. When we are assailed by grave temptations of mind and body, we should abandon all else and let the

> anchor sink deep into the ground, which means perfect trust in God's fidelity, in God's faithfulness. If only we could seize the anchor at the time of our death and so die in perfect hope and trust, what a blessed death it would be.[28]

Remember Melody and so many of your loved ones. They dropped their anchor in Jesus and held on to the rope of undying faith in the middle of the storm.

But wait a minute, weren't we to speak of four ships in a storm? We have only mentioned three thus far.

The first ship was the ship of denial: not coming to grips with reality, trying to sail around the storm of sickness and death and finding ourselves hundreds of miles off course, lost and disillusioned and greatly depressed, out of touch.

The second ship moves straight into the storm, but having nothing to secure us from the furious tempest, we land hard, crushed against the shore, without hope, wounded and in need of healing.

The third ship, where we ground our anchor in God and find safety in Christ Jesus in spite of the storm, seems to be best of all, for though battered by the storm, we can hold our ground in the midst, for our anchor holds and grips the solid rock.

But now to the fourth ship in the storm.

This was a time of trial for Jesus. The Pharisees had decided that Jesus was demon-possessed. If he could cast out devils he must be chief of devils.

Jesus replied, a house divided against itself cannot stand. Will Satan work against Satan?

His relatives had said he was beside himself. He was mad, insane.

His manner of teaching had changed. Since the people did not understand, he wanted them to see without perceiving and hear without understanding. His teaching was cloaked in parables.

His disciples got the real scoop. He explained it all to them. He was as a sower who goes out to sow. Much of the seed would fail. Success was a great way off. The kingdom would indeed be marvelous eventually, but what they represented and saw in the beginning would be weak and small.

His heavy-hearted disciples left the populous side of the lake with him to cross over into remote semi-pagan retirement. The miracle in the storm was designed to encourage them to hold on. They found themselves, as every church and individual has found themselves at one time or another, far from the shore and tempest-beaten. And what is the storm? It is the stress of adverse circumstances in the direst form.

But Jesus proves master of the forces of nature that would try to overwhelm the disciples. He gives them hope while they are in the storm.

"Why are you so fearful? Have ye not yet faith in me?" Here we see a picture of the weariness of the great teacher when the long day is over and the multitude is dismissed. He retreats across the sea, without preparation, and as he sinks to sleep on the cushion in the stern of the ship, he seems undisturbed by the raging tempest or waves that beat into the boat. Jesus is too exhausted to move; he is worn out.

His disciples are reluctant to arouse him until the peril is extreme and the boat is filling with water. When they do cry out, there is the presumption that expresses terror and perhaps dread that they are at the point of perishing while he seems unconcerned.

But his calm and masterful words quell the tempest. God is the anchor. He was the anchor of your loved one, the outside stabilizer of your life. Hold on.

No sooner does the storm cease than the waters, commonly seething for many hours afterwards, grow calm almost immediately.

And the picture is completed by the notion of their new dread. They now fear the supernatural man who replaces terror amid the convulsions of nature. And they were filled with awe and said to one another, "Who then is this, that even the wind and the sea obey him?"

On this voyage of life, Jesus is our companion. Nevertheless, we are storm-tossed and in danger. For although we are his, the conditions of life are unmitigated, the winds are wild, the waves are merciless, and our boat is cruelly tormented. But we are safe in him.

The true lesson of the miracle is that we should trust him whose care fails not and whom we should approach in direst perils without panic. "Be still and know that I am God."

You have a ministry: to quiet the storm of others through your faith. I have watched you at the bedside. You've got it going on. Now pass it on. Work with those who are going through the valley.

Storytelling is a spiritual act, an attempt to find meaning in life's random events. Ninety-four percent of people dealing with pain and illness and disability said over and over again they want more spiritual help from their health-care professionals. Why? Because they are in the middle of the storm, and they need something to hold on to. An anchor. You'd better call your pastor. I'll feel free to call on you because I know you've been there and stood in the midst of the storm. Battered, tear-blinded sometimes, but you stood there, praise God!

People want confidants, confessors, helpers, supporters. Talk slowly, listen patiently.

Most of all, they want people who will listen, especially when they start asking, "Why? Why me? Why now?" They don't necessarily want answers. Most people don't ask such questions unless they already know the answers. They want validation that they already figured it out.

But sometimes they want and need something specific. Perhaps forgiveness, or the reassurance that it wasn't their fault that they got cancer. Healing often hinges on forgiveness. The search for meaning in the midst of the storm is entirely personal. Their spiritual helper is the one who simply comes along for the ride.

But this isn't a passive role. Some patients need coaxing, confirmation that it's OK for them to express their spiritual feelings. Help with life, reviewing, renewing vows, partaking in rituals.

"[Jesus] said to them, 'Why are you afraid? Have you still no faith?' And they were filled with great awe and said to one another, 'Who then is this, that even the wind and the sea obey him?'" (Mark 4:40–41).

What should you say? Nothing. You know how to listen and hold hands. That means so much. The hymnist puts it this way: "In times like these you need a savior. . . . Be very sure your anchor holds and grips the solid rock."[29]

Four ships in the middle of a storm. True love is a painful embrace. This is the way out of a storm.

*Preached December 29, 2002*

# *It's Like a Rocking Chair*

> Fret not thyself because of evildoers, neither be thou envious against the workers of iniquity. For they shall soon be cut down like the grass, and wither as the green herb.
>
> —Psalm 37:1–3 KJV

It's like a rocking chair.

What is like a rocking chair? The answer to this question is our focal point, but let us allow the unfolding message to answer the question. By way of introduction let's look at an everyday experience we all share.

Every now and then the accumulation of trash and half-used items in our garage just has to be cleared away and disposed of, doesn't it? Some of the stuff just has to go. Things like old magazines, newspapers saved for a paper drive that never materialized, boxes that might be used someday, scraps of lumber from by-gone projects, and sacks of outgrown clothing. They all get piled up in every available space in the garage. And finally we can bear it no more. The day inevitably comes when we just have to sort things out and discard a lot of stuff we saved for many years.

Our lives are often like our garages. They are filled with enormous accumulations of unproductive stuff, of dated thinking, biased attitudes, and unhelpful behavior patterns from our past that just need to be cleared away and disposed of.

But the greatest time-wasting, energy-sapping item we have accumulated in our minds and spirits in useless abundance is worry.

So let us consider worry for a little while. Let's list some of our worries. We worry about our health. We worry about families. We worry about finishing the many tasks before us. We worry about our finances, our economic security, and the list goes on. And over in a dark corner of our soul's garage we worry what people think about us. There are other private worries too numerous to mention.

The point is this: All of us carry around a superabundant supply of worries, too many worries, and many of them need to be thrown away. Most of them could be thrown away, and we'd be better off without them. And at the top of our worry mountain are these chief anxieties: What happens next in my life? Will it be for good or ill? How shall I live through another difficult circumstance, another test? Worry, worry, worry.

Listen to the sages speaking about worry and anxiety. It was wise Plato who penned these words two millennia ago: "Nothing in the affairs of men and women is worthy of great anxiety." Plato is right. But we seem not to be able to stop worrying. We are shackled by it. We are deadlocked in it.

One could understand worrying about the unpredictable, but we even worry about predictable events that we know are going to happen. Dispose of this fruitless worrying about the predictable.

Writer Thomas Carlyle once built a soundproof room in his home in London so he could work without interference from outside noises. His neighbor had a rooster that crowed several times every day and night. Carlyle protested to the neighbor, and the man replied that his rooster crowed only three times daily. "Certainly that couldn't be considered a great annoyance." But Carlyle replied, "If you only knew what I suffer waiting for that rooster to crow, you'd know why it disturbs me so." Isn't this our way as well? We anticipate trouble and waste time waiting for it and worrying about it. We even wait anxiously for the predictable to happen. We know in advance that it will bother us, so it depletes our energies and dissipates our strength even before the rooster crows.

Sometime in the nineteenth century, the Reverend Sam Jones was staying overnight with one of his parishioners. During the night, he heard his host walking the floor. Pastor Jones called out to him and said, "What is the matter, brother?"

The parishioner replied that he had a note falling due the next day, and he didn't have the money to pay it.

Reverend Jones asked him what time it was, and he replied, "Twelve midnight."

The pastor then said, "Brother, go to bed and let the other fellow walk the floor the rest of the night. He's the one who will lose and really has cause to worry, when he discovers you can't pay him in the morning."

The pastor was right. Most of our worries are borrowed from some other day.

And isn't it true that some of us worry about mountains we will never have to climb, about streams we will never have to cross, and about situations we will never have to meet? We need to remind ourselves that living a day at a time refers just as much to yesterday as it does to tomorrow.

It's like a rocking chair. Worry is like a rocking chair. Take this little quotation with you and think of it whenever you feel worry and anxiety coming over you. Worry is like a rocking chair. It gives you something to do, but it doesn't get you anywhere.

Now we come to David's words of assurance: "Fret not thyself because of evildoers, neither be thou envious against the workers of iniquity. For they shall soon be cut down like the grass, and wither as the green herb."

"Fret not thyself because of evildoers. . . ." This sentence reads slightly differently in the original Hebrew. There, "fret not thyself" is translated "heat not thyself because of evildoers." To worry is to be heated up. In other words, don't break out into a sweat because of evildoers, because of people who won't give you eye contact, because of people who won't speak to you, because of people who prosper at your expense on your job. You are merely hurting yourself by allowing them to worry you. Don't heat yourself up over them. Dispose of that worry. Throw it away. Don't let it get the upper hand at your expense.

So many times we worry because we see no correlation between our good conduct and the unrighteous conditions surrounding us, pushing us down. We worry about this.

Aren't there times when we run into the buzz saw of adversity, unjust criticism, and mounting difficulties? We feel poor in spirit. Jesus said, "Blessed are the poor in spirit. . . . Theirs is the kingdom of God."

King David says when we are poor in spirit, heat not thyself over evildoers. Fret not over them. He answers the question of the why of trouble by assuring us that godless prosperity will always be brief prosperity, and that well-doing will lead to well-being. He exhorts us to patient trust and the sure blessings thereof. Infinite love rules, and righteousness is always gain, and sin is always loss. This is grandly and eternally true. David also sings the Old Testament song of deliverance, which promised material blessings as the result of spiritual faithfulness.

But, you see, the cross of Jesus Christ was needed before the mystery of righteous suffering could be fully elucidated, so the psalmist's solution is only provisional. Fret not. We need to hear from Jesus. "If I be lifted up, I'll draw all men unto me. I'll draw by my example. In this world you will have tribulation, but be of good cheer. I have overcome the world."

Throw your best soil toward growing a nobler crop. "Fret not thyself. Be not envious. The workers of iniquity shall soon be cut down like the grass, and wither as the green herb."

Here we have the picture of herbage withering as soon as it is cut under the fierce heat of the eastern sun. Why then should we blaze with indignation when so much hotter a glow will dry up the cut grass? Let it wave in brief glory, unmeddled with by us. The scythe and the sun will soon make an end of it.

Do not let the prosperity of unworthy people shake your faith in God's governance nor fling you into an unwholesome heat, because God will sweep away the anomaly in due time.

Don't get all heated up, for worry is like a rocking chair. It gives you something to do, but it just doesn't get you anywhere.

Trust in the Lord and do good. Follow faithfulness. Let your political behavior make a difference in this world and nation. Do good by feeding the poor. Feed the poor. Our present formula for figuring the poverty line dates back to 1963. In 1963 the bare-bones amount the federal government estimated it cost a family of four to feed itself was then multiplied by three, based on the assumption that poor families spent this amount on food. The food formula has not changed in thirty-nine years. We know that though food has had the lowest inflation rate since 1963, it now takes about 20 percent (a multiplier of five, not three) of the average poor person's income to feed the family.

But our federal government is loathe to adjust the poverty line formula because this would mean recognizing that many more people are poor than we currently claim—hence the need for more assistance.

Trust in the Lord and do good, and verily shall thou be fed. What is the answer? Remember Sam Jones's advice to the parishioner? If you can correct a wrong then do so, and go ahead with the business of living today.

Finally, let's look at the story of Willis H. Carrier, who founded the Carrier air-conditioning company. Years earlier, when he worked for the Buffalo Forge Company, they sent him to install a glass-cleaning device in a plate glass factory in Missouri. The device, which cost twenty thousand dollars, was still in the experimental stage of development. He was worried, but in time his common sense told him worry wasn't getting him anywhere. He took two steps that saved the day.

First, he analyzed the situation fearlessly and honestly. Now that he was no longer paralyzed with fear he could think clearly. Second, he saw that by spending another five thousand dollars he could make the machine work properly. Throw your soil toward a nobler crop. He did so, saved his reputation, and enabled the Buffalo Forge Company to prosper. What does this teach us?

- Life is experimental, not fixed.
- Analyze your worry calmly, fearlessly, and honestly so you can think clearly.

- You will discover that much of our worry is refusal to accept something that cannot be altered from the past, something unpleasant in the present, or possibly contemplated in the future.
- Worry paralyzes. Get rid of it. Accept the facts and accept the forgiveness of God. God is more ready to forgive us than we are to forgive ourselves.

This is the way we can all break free from the burden of the past and the burden of the future and live creatively today.

*Preached November 10, 2002*

# Part 5
## *Renewal*

Well, we know we all have room for improvement. And we always will. We all have secret sins and thoughts we're not eager to share, even with God. Even in our most private, confessional moments, we still hesitate to reveal all about ourselves.

Because we don't always feel cleansed and right with ourselves or others or with God, we sometimes put our heads down and shuffle along a course that we follow without much conscious choosing, a course that quite often breeds isolation instead of community and selfishness instead of generosity and sacrifice.

How shall we overcome? I say again, we already have. We have overcome through Jesus Christ.

And we can be renewed. Granted, renewal requires our commitment to all our relationships—to our relationship with those in our lives, with God, and with ourselves. To be renewed takes vigilance and dedication, faith and forgiveness, balance and grace.

We may have to learn some lessons over and over along our way. But if we keep heading down the path that Jesus and Martin lit like beacons, we will be renewed. As Martin said, we can disagree with someone, but we must love them for their personhood. And if we relate at this soulful level of common personhood and love, we will find peace in those relationships and we will all be renewed in dignity.

Freedom comes from faith. Our most valuable assets are not our possessions. People can repossess or rob us of our things. Our fear of losing our material worth shackles us to a life measured by an inferior currency. But no one can take away our faith, and knowing that brings us ultimate freedom. Faith allows us to take on great challenges and brings unsurpassed renewal.

Each day is precious beyond measure, for we don't know when it will be our last. Don't wait to help and heal. Don't let the sun go down on forgiveness. Carry the spirit and the peace of the Sabbath with you; it's essential for renewal and the fullness of living.

In these concluding messages, we trace the power given us to bear witness and help those in darkness, even though our own prospects for overcoming look dim, and night swiftly approaches in our lives. We are Christ's light in the world. We find our illumination in Christ, who saw people blinded by many unwarranted injustices and oppressive conditions. Yet he always sought to mend broken relationships, before night fell and no one could work.

Then through the eyes of Robert Fulghum, we are renewed with a lighthearted, yet very profound view of the meaning of Christmas. Here we find a way to overcome the cynicism this festive occasion sometimes evokes.

If we are to overcome, we need to acknowledge the difficulties of forgiving others for past wrongs, both personal and societal. Can we couple the concept of forgiveness with a theological understanding of reconciliation through prayer? To forgive is at least as essential as daily bread, yet we have a deeper hunger! We long to have our consciences clear in our relationships with God, our families, friends, and neighbors. Yes, we even long to be reconciled to those from whom we are estranged, our enemies. Only then can we be at peace again!

Finally, we come full circle, from the communal to the personal, for it is ultimately in understanding the richness of solitude with God that we are renewed and continue life's long journey toward overcoming. *It is a never-ending quest!*

# *It Is Evening!*

> [Jesus said] I must work the works of him that sent me, while it is day: the night cometh, when no man can work.
>
> —John 9:4 KJV

Yes, even now, it is evening.

Let me introduce this message by speaking of author C. S. Lewis, who was born in Belfast, Ireland, in 1898. Lewis was a scholar and layperson who established himself in the fields of medieval and sixteenth-century literature and Christian apologetics. He taught for forty years at Oxford University but, at the last, held the chair in medieval and Renaissance English literature at Cambridge.

His most powerful tools were fantasy and myth. In one of his fantasies, titled *The Great Divorce*,[30] the residents of Graytown live a twilight existence in which evening never advances into night. What a peculiar thought, to live in a place where evening never blends into night.

The residents of Graytown can leave whenever they wish, trading their city for the joys of heaven, but most of them will not. Why? Because they don't want to go to heaven if it means leaving their favorite sins behind. Doesn't this ring a bell in your life and mine? Yes, we too are like the residents of Graytown. We love many of our sins, more than the joys of heaven, so we'll just stay in the evening, the twilight zone.

But then something terrible happens. Graytown's residents learned that it was all over.

Lewis listens to a resident of Graytown:

> *I put my ear close to his mouth. "Speak up," I said.*
>
> *"It will be dark presently," he noted.*
>
> *"You mean the evening is really going to turn into a night in the end?"*
>
> *He nodded.*

Even in Graytown, evening would eventually turn into night, and they feared the night. Yes, Lewis put his finger on our fear. For many can live with the evening, but we don't want it to pass into night. We fear the darkness of night and its loneliness. But why do we really fear the night? Not because it is dark or dangerous, but because it brings to us the utter darkness of hell.

But if hell is night, thank God this is only evening. It is only evening, and we, like the residents of Graytown, want to pray that evening never advances into the darkness of night.

Now look at our lives. It's evening for more of us than will admit it. Aren't we going around in circles, procrastinating just a little too much, advancing nowhere?

It is evening. . . . Our day is far spent. Oh, how quickly it came and passed us.

Think about your life. It is evening now. Do you remember when it was all in front of you, when you had the world in your pocket? That was only yesterday. And now it is evening? We are in the twilight zone of our time? It passed us so swiftly, didn't it? We can hardly imagine where the time went.

It is evening, and night is coming. Yes, children and adults fear the darkness, for night is often depicted as a time full of anxiety and dread.

For Jesus, the night represented the end of opportunity, of work, of life. It is evening. The residents of Lewis's Graytown really missed the boat. The night is coming, whether we like it or not, whether we are ready for it or not. Jesus said it, it is already evening.

But don't worry. For Jesus also said, "As long as I am in the world, I am the light of the world" (John 9:5).

In the evening of his life, Jesus was walking along the road, escaping from his enemies at the temple. When he saw a man blind from birth, he stopped, heedless of self-preservation, to heal him.

Now, the disciples didn't think Jesus should stop for the man, figuring that he was a sinner anyway. Their major inquiry was why was the man thrown into this darkness? Why was he blind? They were more concerned with the reasons for his darkness than how they could help him see. They believed that sin was the cause for suffering, a common notion at the time. So they asked Jesus, who sinned? This man or his parents? Who threw him into this evening time of his life, so quickly? Give us a cause, a reason for human suffering and pain. Why should it happen in the good creation and to the people you created?

If we must cope with suffering, who regulates its distribution? It seems so arbitrary, so unfair. So many good people we know are suffering even today. And why is it that so many criminals prosper, almost exempt from pain, while many gentle and innocent people are broken and tortured by constant suffering?

Why, Jesus? It is evening in this man's life, in your life, and in ours. Why? Why do bad things happen to good people? The disciples push on. It is evening in this man's life and in yours and in ours. But since you're going to stop, tell us. Perhaps the blind man was the recipient of punishment for his parents' wrong?

But again, Jesus shakes his head in the negative. No, says Jesus, there is another reason.

We know that all suffering is certainly not hereditary. It doesn't always come because "the fathers have eaten sour grapes and the children's teeth are set on edge."

But it is evening, and the night fast approaches. We need some answers before the darkness engulfs us. We know suffering is often the result of accident or of malice or of a mistake. Maybe his suffering and yours and ours are the shavings and sawdust, the general disorder of the carpenter's workshop, which must be thrown off in making us into God's needful article? Could it be this?

No, neither this man nor his parents sinned. He was born blind so that God's work might be revealed in him.

But let me reverse myself and suggest that there are also times when we do suffer for individual and hereditary sins. By breaking the great moral laws of human life, we constantly involve both ourselves and our children in lifelong suffering.

And we cannot deny that more often than not, our pain and misery are self-inflicted, but we just don't want to own up to it. Sometimes the connection is obscure, yet though everyone else sees the source of our misfortunes in our own careless habit, or indolence, or bad temper, we just cannot! We live in a state of continual denial.

We constantly blame our circumstances on misfortune, bad luck. We blame our intimate partners, even our dearest friends. We are in denial about the cause of our own darkness. We project the fault for our darkness on somebody else. Never on ourselves. That's a total moral eclipse. We must examine ourselves.

But the purpose of our Lord's dialogue with his curious disciples who wondered why the man was blind had another motivation. He wished to warn us all against a curious and uncharitable scrutiny of any man's life to find the cause of his misfortunes. The church of Jesus Christ is concerned about the future, not the past; the dawn, not the darkness.

We, like the disciples, question how a person got himself into trouble but offer little help for getting anybody through and out of trouble. We seek the cause of the suffering in order to blame somebody for what they did. No matter what caused the suffering, it is always with us, and we seek to find in the suffering material and opportunity to work with God to deliver.

God is a worker. He knows he is working in the evening, in the twilight zone. God is doing everything he can. He is carrying the world on toward perfection, and if the world is ever to be perfect, it must be purged from all agony and wretchedness, irrespective of where these come from.

It is evening, for Jesus and the blind man. The enemies of Jesus are in hot pursuit, but Jesus immediately applies himself to the work of healing the blind man. He applies himself to this man's evening situation. He must work the works of him who sent him. By loving that blind man just as the father loved him, and by doing for him just what the father would have done for him, Jesus was God's agent.

And so are we. We do the works of God when in our measure we become the eyes of the blind, the feet of the lame, the help of the helpless.

We cannot lay our hands on the diseased and heal them. We cannot give sight to the blind and make a person feel, "This is God's power reaching me. This is God stopping by me and caring for my infirmity." But we can cause people to feel that God is thinking of them and has sent help through us to them.

If we will only be humble enough to run the risk of failure. If we will only take by the hand those who are ill and strive to better them, then these persons will think of God gratefully.

Sometimes we feel, confronted as we are with a whole world full of deep-rooted and inveterate evils, it is useless giving assistance to an individual here and there. It is like trying to dry up the ocean with a sponge. But Jesus helped just as he passed by.

Don't wait until you can do all things on a great scale and attack the evils of human life with elaborate machinery. Jesus did not busy himself forming charitable institutions. Jesus did not convene assemblies to consider the relief of the poor. He did not found orphanages or hospitals, but as he passed by he saw one blind man and judged his call sufficiently urgent.

It is evening. The enemies are coming near me. I must work the works of him that sent me. The night cometh.

"The gates of it shall not be shut at all by day: for there shall be no night there" (Rev. 21:25 KJV).

*Preached October 4, 1998*

# *I'm It!*

Robert Fulghum tells of a Sunday afternoon before Christmas. It was a rainy, windy, cold day and he was gloomy—too many things to do, too much bad news on all fronts. No Christmas spirit. But suddenly he heard a pounding on his door, and when he opened it there stood a small person in a Santa Claus mask, holding a brown paper bag, and saying, in accented English, "Trick or treat!" His next question was, "Want to hear some caroling?" Fulghum eventually recognized the boy as a neighbor, Hong Duc, one of the children of a refugee family.

Hong Duc didn't need any other voices to sing with him, and he immediately launched into "Jingle Bells," "Hark the Herald Angels Sing," and finally, "a soft-voiced, reverential singing of 'Silent Night.' . . . Hong Duc, the one-man choir, delivering Christmas door to door."

Fulghum writes: "God, it is said, once sent a child upon a starry night that the world might know hope and joy. I am not sure that I quite believe that or that I believe in all the baggage heaped upon that story during 2,000 years: But I am sure that I believe in Hong Duc and his one-boy Christmas choir shouting "trick or treat" door to door. . . . Through a child I have been treated to Christmas.[31]

What do we learn from Hong Duc? First, when God measures a person, he puts the tape measure around a person's heart. So celebrate this season by giving the gift of yourself. Say to yourself, "I'm it," and remember your hope, your peace, your love (all gifts from God) will outshine any purchased present on Christmas. The Scripture puts it simply: seek peace and pursue it.

Second, if you suffer from Christmas blues, remember no one day is ever perfect. There will be detractors everywhere trying to spoil your life. Don't let them! Dismiss from your mind the hurtful comments or stinging remarks. Let your brightness make peace out of chaos. Behold the star. Be the star that shines and sheds glowing light to dispel the darkness of any mishap.

Third, the great gift you can give is to let the disappointments slide by, the irritations go unrecognized, and replace them with smiles and hugs. Ask yourself, *How can I make this situation better?*

Fourth, love unconditionally. Say a silent "I love you" to those you meet, and you will know the warm, glowing, peaceful love of God. This is the greatest gift the world has ever known.

For unto us a child is born.

Isaiah is terribly upset with King Ahaz, king of Judah. Ahaz has neighboring enemies, Syria and Samaria, of whom he is unwarrantedly afraid. So he decides to join in an alliance with a more ruthless enemy, the Assyrian monarch Tiglathpileser, to protect his province of Judah from Syria and Samaria. He could have entered into an alliance with his neighbors Syria and Samaria against Assyria and saved the whole region, but King Ahaz couldn't see that far, as he was only looking out for number one. Sound familiar?

Isaiah said, "You're wrong, the Assyrians cannot protect you, but God can. You are in the messianic line, a part of the house of David." But King Ahaz would not listen. He invited the Assyrians to come, and subsequently the Galilean provinces in the north are depopulated and we see the beginning of the end. The king caved in to selfishness.

But Isaiah still has hope.

There are lessons to be learned here. Learn to rate your enemies at their proper value. King Ahaz was more afraid of Syria and Samaria, smaller nations than Assyria, the larger one with more grave designs. Let the small ones go.

We all need a central authority, a core, and we have one: for unto us a child is born. Without this central core we are devoid of breadth of view or length of patience. Everything that ain't nailed down is coming loose. Nothing is holding us together, no covenant consensus. This is our problem. For when you really know God's love, central and supreme, you can fling prejudices and superstitions to the winds. And when we know God reigns, it gives us quietness and makes us truly free and secure. I'm it. For unto us a child is born, a son is given.

Don't be a fatalist. King Ahaz was. Fulghum was moving close to being one until Hong Duc came along. Fatalism means resignation to fate. Fatalism is the characterless condition that reduces us to our blues.

Hong Duc is trying to help us know God intimately again. God comes among us to be heard and seen and handled by us that our hearts may learn his heart and know his love, unafraid of his majesty, like Hong Duc.

It is not enough to know that God reigneth but to know what kind of God he is who reigneth. Hong Duc says, "If you're looking for Christmas, I'm it!"

*Preached December 21, 1997*

# *To Be at Peace Again*

## Forgiveness

Allow me to address the tender and sensitive work of forgiveness. More specifically, I speak to the quest of almost every human soul who has had to live with alienation and estrangement from friends and comrades. Certainly we all pray to be at peace again with ourselves and with each other.

To help us, let's take a look at the Lord's Prayer, which is really the disciples' prayer taught to them by Jesus Christ. The fifth petition of that prayer is, Forgive us our debts as we forgive our debtors.

First, some general thoughts about this petition, our quest for forgiveness.

As Jesus lays out an order for prayer, this quest for forgiveness immediately follows the petition to give us this day our daily bread. It almost seems that the Lord is implying that we do not live to fill our physical appetites alone, for even when that is done, we have a deeper hunger, a desire to have our consciences clear in our relationships with God and those around us. Give us our daily bread, and forgive our debts? But to whom are we indebted?

We have a primary misunderstanding regarding this passage. We think it only implies that we concern ourselves with a sociological breach of a social contract. We think it only means we need to be forgiven of our debts to each other. The problem for most of us is that we fail to see that it is not just the neighbor but also God, to whom we are in deeper debt. We have sinned against the author, creator, and redeemer of the universe. This petition reminds us of our constant tendency to sin against God, as we refuse to forgive each other.

So we start renewal this way: Forgive us our debts to you, Lord, as we forgive our debts to each other. We are all indebted first and foremost to God.

Here, as we approach the throne of God in prayer, Jesus is showing us how to differentiate between theoretical forgiveness and factual forgiveness. Certain things in life and faith are absolute, but about others we have some liberty; they are relative.

The first absolute is this: forgiveness is a favor extended to us by God, not a whimsical essence we can lay claim to whenever we wish it. In other words, I can't say, "I think I'll lay claim to God's forgiveness today."

It's not just ours to claim so easily, whenever we wish to. It is a gift of God through Jesus Christ. If we really fervently wish to have forgiveness of our debts, our personal acts of disobedience against the will of God, we first have to dispose of all enmity before bringing our oblation to the altar, before voicing our petitions in prayer. Now, that's a tough assignment!

"Pastor, do you mean that I am to come to the altar with charity and goodwill toward others . . . that I can't reserve a little grudge against anybody?" That's it, that's the tough assignment: we are to be at peace again with all our neighbors.

We are to come with a heart clear of ill will. "Do you mean that I have to be kind to those I don't like, if I expect such kindness from God toward me? I don't know if I can do that," we reply.

Well, that seems to be what this prayer is teaching us. For if we come to the prayer moment, whether in church or in our home, while retaining any uncharitable inclinations toward any other person, we deal falsely with God and hereby forfeit all hope of mercy and favor from him.

It's right there, clear as day: Forgive us our debts as we forgive our debtors. This is a reminder of the condition upon which God will extend forgiveness to us. It does have strings attached.

We are the children of our heavenly parent, and we are in debt to God. Each day of our lives, our debts, our sins, express themselves in our unwillingness to forgive others. This petition presupposes that sin which remains unremitted has an indelible place in divine remembrance. These sins are registered, tallied by God.

Let me try a contemporary example. When I check into a hotel and stay a few days, a record of my stay is kept by the hotel management and I am hardly aware of it. My telephone calls are charged on a daily basis, so are my restaurant charges, and so on, but then the moment of truth comes. It's checkout time on the day of my departure, and the clerk, representing management, shares with me the totality of my daily charges. Sometimes we can't believe we have talked that much or eaten that much, but there it is, recorded, tallied in black and white. It is so easy to run up the charges, because they were incurred at different times during our stay, but they do add up, and the question is, can we pay the bill when it is time to leave the hotel?

Life is like that. Our daily debts against the account of God's love, our sins are constantly being recorded. In fact, they record themselves. We don't notice them, we ignore them early on, but our sins are adding up as we pass through the turnstile of this mortal order we call life.

Take another illustration—the cash register at the checkout counter at the grocery. When you're passing down the aisle, picking up this or that it doesn't seem like much, but when the bill is tallied, often we have insufficient funds and we have to take some items back to the shelves because we can't afford all of this stuff.

In this life we are running up an enormously expensive tab with God that has to be paid. So when we get to the checkout counters of our lives, we cry out, "Forgive us our debts, Lord, let us be at peace with you again."

But you ask, how is my sin debt, and how can it be satisfied? Two questions in one statement. Let's separate them. First, how is my sin debt? Sin is a failed obligation to God that I cannot deny, ignore, transfer, or run away from. It's going to be checkout time one of these days for all of us. And the bill we are running up against God is enormous.

But now to the second question. I know what the debt is, but how is it ever to be satisfied? Not by my repentance nor by my good works nor by any amount of my seeking and striving. But solely by the grace of God, forgiving my debt for the sake of Jesus Christ our Lord and my savior.

Now let us move from forgiving our debts to the next phrase, "as we forgive." This seems to imply that forgiveness of our neighbors is the mandatory condition, the prerequisite for God's forgiveness of us. It seems to imply that we cannot lift a genuine prayer for our own pardon from God unless we cultivate a forgiving spirit toward those from whom we feel separated spiritually. Are we praying for God's favor, which will allow us to be at peace again with those from whom we have spiritual and social separation? These are the critical questions we need to face.

The pardon of God is always linked with repentance of sins, and one of the sins for which we all need to repent before we can ever ask to be pardoned is the sin of an unforgiving spirit.

Faith in God's mercy is incompatible with unmercifulness in ourselves toward others. Or to put it another way, gratitude to God for pardon received or expected for ourselves has to prompt in us forgiveness of others, including those who have wronged us.

If you don't feel like forgiving, you haven't been pardoned. And the person who will not forgive forsakes the spirit of the gospel of Christ. The person who does not forgive will soon lose the sense and enjoyment of God's pardon. To be pardoned simply means that I am at peace again with God and with you.

This petition in the Lord's Prayer simply states that we should treat everybody with dignity as persons of worth. In other words, there are rights which belong to each of us that every other person in the world is under divine obligation to honor and respect. It also suggests that we not seek restitution beyond what is necessary for our security; restitution should not be based on resentment.

"Forgive us our debts as we forgive our debtors."

Forgive quickly, settle, and agree. Paul said, "Do not let the sun go down on your wrath . . . for when we do not forgive one another right away, when we hold grudges we have heavy burdens, weariness, fear, a sense of perplexity, and a cold and ungodly feeling of hatred." Give us the ability to forgive each day. Don't hold it. Lose the grudge today. Settle and agree today.

A wise old tutor took a stroll through the forest with a curious youth by his side. The tutor suddenly stopped and pointed to four plants close at hand. The first, a tiny sprout just coming out of the earth. The second had rooted itself quite firmly in the fertile soil. The third was a small shrub. The fourth had grown into a well-developed tree. The teacher said to his youthful companion, "Pull up this first plant." A tiny plant. The youth pulled it up easily with his fingers. "Now pull up the second." With slight effort the plant came up root and all. The third was a small shrub. First one hand, then it took both to get the plant to yield to all of his strength. And now, the fourth. The youth grasped the trunk with all his might, but hardly a leaf shook. "I cannot move it."

"Just so, my son, with all our bad habits. When they are young and small we can cast them out, but when they are fully grown, they cannot be uprooted." Do not let the sun go down on your wrath if you would have peace again.

How do I forgive? Frederick Buechner suggests that to forgive somebody is to say, "In one way or another you have done something unspeakable, and by all rights I should call it quits between us. Both my pride and my principles demand no less. However, although I make no guarantees that I will be able to forget what you've done, and though we may both carry the scars for life, I refuse to let it stand between us. I still want you for my friend."[32]

To accept forgiveness means that a person must say I've done something unspeakable that needs to be forgiven. Then both parties must swallow the same thing: their pride.

"Forgive us our debts as we forgive our debtors." What Jesus is apparently saying is that it is pride which keeps us from forgiving, the same pride that keeps us from accepting forgiveness.

We are asking God to please help us do something about this chilling, death-producing pride of ours, for we are self-destructing in our self-righteousness.

What are the benefits of forgiveness? When somebody we've wronged forgives us, we are spared the dull and self-diminishing throb of a guilty conscience. When we forgive somebody who has wronged us, we are spared the dismal corrosion of bitterness and wounded pride. The greatest benefit: for both persons, forgiveness means the freedom again to be at peace inside their own skins and to be glad in each other's presence.

Redwood trees stand three hundred feet high and live twenty-five hundred years. Their roots are interlocked. They stand together, supporting one another. Let us live together and have peace again.

*Preached July 10, 1994*

# *We Can Be Renewed*

## Solitude

> Do not be conformed to this world, but be transformed by the renewing of your minds, so that you may discern what is the will of God—what is good and acceptable and perfect.
>
> —Romans 12:2–3

Allow me to employ as a springboard for this message these words of Paul, from his letter to the Romans, chapter 12. He says, in essence, if our lives are to know regeneration, revitalization, resurgence, and indeed renewal, we need to give God some prime time in our daily schedule of hectic involvements. Yes, it is possible for us to be renewed, writes Paul. But listen to his warning. "Do not be conformed to this world, but be transformed by the renewing of your minds."

I have been reading some of the writings of Father Thomas Merton, a graduate of Columbia University, who entered the Roman Catholic Trappist Abbey at the age of twenty-three in 1938. He probably has done more to change our attitudes toward spirituality, monasticism, and contemplation than any other twentieth-century religious thinker. Notice how he echoes the sentiments of the apostle Paul, who speaks to us regarding nonconformity to the common standards, folkways, and mores of this world in which we live and move, when he writes:

> The world of men and women has forgotten the joys of silence, the peace of solitude which is necessary to some

> extent for the fullness of human living. . . . If a person is locked out of their solitude, that person ceases to be truly human. One becomes a kind of automaton, living without joy, because they have lost all spontaneity. Such a person is no longer moved from within, but only from outside themselves. Such a person no longer makes decisions for himself but lets them be made for him.

Sounds like Paul's sentiments, don't they? "Do not be conformed to this world, but be transformed by the renewing of your minds. . . ."

Father Merton continues on the subject of solitude: "Such a person no longer acts upon the outside world but lets it act upon him. He is propelled through life by a series of collisions with outside forces, a being without a purpose and without any deeply valid response to reality."[33]

We actually try to avoid solitude. We enter our empty apartments and flick on the TV. We don't like solitude. We have to have sound. An evening alone? Not hardly, we quickly call a friend to go to a movie or to the shopping mall.

But this is not the way our God designed it in the beginning. We've been tampering with his script.

The creation story tells us that after six days, God himself rested from his labors. Can we at least learn to rest from ours? On the Sabbath, it is time to redefine and renew ourselves inwardly. Jesus said we were not made for the Sabbath, the Sabbath was made for us. Do we really know what that means?

The Pharisees would not let one carry a burden on the Sabbath day, and they had something there.

Stop a minute and gather yourselves together. Observe the Sabbath so you can be refreshed, revived, renewed again according to the regular rhythms of the universe—the natural ebb and flow of the tides of your life and mine.

The Sabbath was set aside by God for us to provide us with a little grace, the grace of an acknowledged break from the grind of existence: a time of fellowship for those supported by God's power and love through the week.

But let us not confine ourselves to a weekly Sabbath. My God, we need to claim our gratitude for grace every day of our lives. We need to be renewed daily. But our agenda is already laid out for the week with plans through Friday at least. We have to arise at 6:30 a.m. just to get a few things accomplished.

Because there is not time for centering—that's what solitude provides—there is no center, no direction in our lives.

When we have no direction, we are tossed and turned by any whimsical objective, any idolatrous worship, including the worship of ourselves. Our lives become scattered and full of stress. Without a center, without direction, we allow the world to squeeze us into a mold. Like Jell-O, we fit nicely into predetermined forms and shapes. Or as Merton writes, we become like robots, always responding to outside stimuli, outside pressure, outside expectations—in other words, the world affects us far more than we affect the world.

When we are locked out of our spiritual solitude—no Sabbath moments in our day, no times of grace—we are like people who have lost the keys to their houses. We cannot gain entrance into a space that is ours where we can grow in awareness of who and whose we are.

Solitude allows God's spirit within us to become the person we were created to be so that we respond to the world's needs in ways that are not somebody else's but our own.

We are transformed by the renewal of our minds, that we may prove what is the will of God, as Paul asserts.

Up to chapter 12 in Paul's Epistle to the Romans, he had traveled the theoretical theological journey. He had discussed in exquisite form the thorny issues of righteousness, sanctification, and our final redemption. Now he moves from the theoretical to the practical.

He speaks of the journey of each individual soul. The Christian, says Paul, filled with the knowledge of eternal love, is not to dream but to serve God, with the mercies of God's love for him being the ground of his motivation.

We are just to do right, to do justly, to love mercy, and to walk humbly with our God. We are able to do this because we are in grace, rooted in the bedrock realities of God's divine truth and abiding love for us.

Paul gets more specific about renewal in these four points in Thessalonians, applying saving truth to common life.

1. Aspire to live quietly, to mind your own affairs.
2. Work with your hands so that you may behave properly toward outsiders and be dependent on no one.
3. Seriously apply the details of your lives to the will of God.
4. Renew your mind that you may prove what is the will of God, what is good and acceptable and perfect.

Now for the practical application of this message regarding our need for inward renewal today. We can be renewed if we do not conform to this world. The Sabbath rest, the timeout period for grace, is designed to reduce stress. We can be renewed. The first step in becoming more peaceful is to have the humility to admit that usually we create our own stress. But life is not an emergency. What you want is not an emergency.

Now, what is stress? You can't define it, but you know it and can feel it coming on. According to Dr. Richard Carlson, stress is a signal to stop. Let's say you're a jogger and you sprain your ankle. Well, the pain, the stress tells you to stop, sit down, put some ice on it and rest.

Mental stress is the same. *I'm losing it,* you might tell yourself. *I need a break.* Solution? Simple, all of us can do it. Take a few deep breaths, slowly; it will relax you. Drawing in deep breaths slows you down and creates a gap between what's irritating you and your reaction to it.

The solution is to notice what's happening in your head before it has a chance to build up momentum, to snowball.

What are some of the warning signals that stress is beginning to snowball in your life and soul?

1. Nervousness, anxiety, or irritability throughout the day.
2. Under- or overeating, gaining or losing weight.
3. Feeling lethargic, fatigued, or weighed down by demands.

4. Having no time for fun or seeing friends.
5. Concentrating on the negatives.
6. Wishing your life was different.

How can we be renewed? Deal with this reality. There will be chaotic moments in your life and mine, when all we can say is, "This is just one of those days." But you can practice being serene in the midst of chaos. Ask yourself, *Will this issue that I'm stressed out over really matter one month from now*? And suppose it is a big problem. Isn't it normal to be stressed over big problems? Yes, absolutely. But this is funny. Have you noticed that we handle major crises, big problems, better than we do waiting in a grocery line? Isn't that pathetic? But it's true.

Look what happens when a parent dies. Kids fly home. There are prayers, togetherness, love. Or after a flood or earthquake, people come together with incredible strength. They go without sleep, risk their lives to help a stranger. Yet we flip out when we are waiting in a grocery line.

How can we be better stress managers? I once read this list of helpful suggestions:

- Somewhere understand the difference between real and self-created stress. See that you're doing some of it to yourself. If you can't see this, you'll be doomed to the tiresome attempt to prove to yourself that life is always hard.
- Live in the present moment.
- Go with the flow and let go of problems.
- Practice being patient.
- Surrender to the fact that life isn't fair.
- Choose your battles wisely.
- Set aside quiet time daily.
- Practice random acts of kindness.
- Take a deep breath before you speak.
- Write down your five most stubborn positions, and see if you can soften them.
- Learn to ignore your negative thoughts.

- Do one thing at a time. Give up the idea that more is better.
- When you're in a bad mood, it is not the time to think about your life problems. Just focus on tiny attitude shifts.
- Realize you're never more than a thought away from a transformation. Ask God to nudge you in that direction.
- Just start catching yourself. "There I go again." Do that a few hundred times, and I guarantee you you'll make good shifts in the way you live.

"Do not be conformed to this world, but be transformed by the renewing of your minds." We can be renewed.

Make some sand castles.

Christi, Andrew, and Katie, ages thirteen, twelve, and ten, were at the beach with their dad. "I'm bored," Katie said. "Daddy, make a sand castle with me."

"Not now, honey, I'm resting."

"But you made sand castles with Christie and Andy." That got him.

Slowly as parents, we become less passionate. We have that "been there, done that" attitude when our youngest children come along. But she got him. "I'll build one with you," he said. And out of all that happened that day, the one memory that stuck gloriously in his mind was building a sand castle with his little daughter.

Every day, in a figurative sense, I am making sand castles with those I love. I have only a short time in which to make them before the tide comes in and washes our efforts all away, for time is the most essential ingredient in making a sand castle.

I regret all those missed opportunities when I should have made a sand castle but instead nestled my feet comfortably in the sand. There is only a little time to create memories and share moments together before the tide comes in and washes it all away.

"Do not be conformed to this world, but be transformed by the renewing of your minds."

This is the Sabbath. Why don't you build some sand castles with someone you love today?

*Preached September 10, 2000*

# *Notes*

1. Martin Luther King Jr. *A Testament of Hope—The Essential Writings of Martin Luther King, Jr.*, ed. James M. Washington (Harper & Row Publishers, 1986), 52.

2. Ibid., 555.

3. Ibid., 556.

4. Ibid.

5. Ibid., 557.

6. Ibid.

7. Ibid., 558.

8. Ibid.

9. Ibid., 560.

10. Ibid., 565.

11. Ibid., 518.

12. Ibid.

13. Ibid., 519.

14. Ibid.

15. Ibid.

16. Ibid., 523.

17. The Booker T. Washington Papers, open book edition, Louis Harland, desk edition—John W. Blassingame, copyright 1972, University of Illinois.

18. *Daily Readings from Spiritual Classics*, ed. Paul Ofstedal (Minneapolis: Augsburg Fortress, 1990), 39.

19. Ibid., 275.

20. *Christian Century* article by Robert Bellah, Prof. of Sociology, University of California at Berkeley.

21. Robert Fulghum, *It Was on Fire When I Lay Down on It* (New York: Ballentine Books, 1993), 191.

22. Ibid.

23. *Daily Readings from Spiritual Classics*, 30.

24. Robert Fulghum, *All I Really Need to Know I Learned In Kindergarten: Uncommon Thoughts on Common Things* (New York: Ballentine Books, 1991), 9–12.

25. Bruce Barton, *Michael Moncur's (Cynical) Quotations*, quotation #23626; Quotationspage.com.

26. Robert Fulghum, *Uh-Oh: Some Observations from Both Sides of the Refrigerator Door!* (New York: Ballentine Books, 1991), 155–60.

27. *Daily Readings from Spiritual Classics*, 398.

28. *Daily Readings from Spiritual Classics*, 296.

29. Ruth Caye Jones, "In Times Like These," copyright 1944, Singspiration Music (ASCAP), *African American Heritage Hymnal* (Chicago: GIA Publications, Inc., 2001), 309.

30. C. S. Lewis, *The Great Divorce* (New York: Macmillan, 1973).

31. Fulghum, *All I Really Need to Know I Learned In Kindergarten*, 90–93.

32. Frederick Buechner, *Wishful Thinking: A Theological ABC* (San Francisco: HarperSanFrancisco, 1987).

33. *Daily Reading from Spiritual Classics*, 74.